Insider's Guide to School Leadership

Insider's Guide
to School Leadership

GETTING THINGS DONE
WITHOUT LOSING YOUR MIND

Mark F. Goldberg

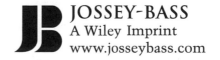

JOSSEY-BASS
A Wiley Imprint
www.josseybass.com

Published by Jossey-Bass
A Wiley Imprint
989 Market Street, San Francisco, CA 94103-1741   www.josseybass.com

Jossey-Bass books and products are available through most bookstores. To contact Jossey-Bass directly call our Customer Care Department within the U.S. at 800-956-7739, outside the U.S. at 317-572-3986, or fax 317-572-4002.

Jossey-Bass also publishes its books in a variety of electronic formats. Some content that appears in print may not be available in electronic books.

Library of Congress Cataloging-in-Publication Data

Goldberg, Mark F., date.
     Insider's guide to school leadership : getting things done without losing your mind / Mark F. Goldberg.— 1st ed.
       p. cm. — (Jossey-Bass education series)
     Includes index.
     ISBN-13: 978-0-7879-8208-9 (alk. paper)
     ISBN-10: 0-7879-8208-3 (alk. paper)
     1. School management and organization. I. Title.
LB2805.G5394 2006
371.2'00973—dc22
                2005024317

Printed in the United States of America
FIRST EDITION
PB Printing   10 9 8 7 6 5 4 3 2 1

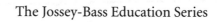

The Jossey-Bass Education Series

CONTENTS

ACKNOWLEDGMENTS

Two distinguished editors made it possible for me to travel around the country over a period of more than ten years to meet and interview leading figures in education as well as many additional successful administrators in school districts near the interview sites. Their strong encouragement and material support were indispensable.

Ron Brandt was for many years a key executive at ASCD. Among his various duties and exceptional talents, he served as director of all of ASCD's publications. He and I met for breakfast in Boston at an ASCD conference and agreed on my doing a series of articles for *Educational Leadership (EL)* on such outstanding educators as James Comer, Dennis Littky, Ted Sizer, Debby Meier, the late Albert Shanker, and John Goodlad. I interviewed each person, usually in his or her office or home, for at least two hours and turned each interview into an article of interest to *EL*'s readers. The series was followed by a summary article titled "Portraits of Educators: Reflections on Eighteen High Achievers" (*Educational Leadership*, May 1995).

My second series of articles was for *Phi Delta Kappan*, under the sponsorship of the late *Pauline Gough*, for many years the *Kappan*'s accomplished and encouraging editor. My agreement with Pauline was somewhat different from the one with Ron Brandt in that we contracted for me to expand the word *educator* to include people in important positions with a serious interest in education. That series of twenty-three articles included in-person interviews with such educators as Carol Gilligan, E. D. Hirsch Jr., and Linda Darling-Hammond, but also with such figures as Mayor Rudolph Giuliani of New York, Mayor Kurt Schmoke of Baltimore, Governor

Lowell Weicker of Connecticut, and the late writer-scientist Stephen Jay Gould. It concluded with an article titled "Leadership in Education: Five Commonalities" (*Phi Delta Kappan,* June 2001).

In all, I published forty-one articles in the two series between 1989 and 2001 and accumulated a great deal of information about leadership and administration, a process that continues to this day as I travel around the country, visit schools, attend conferences, and meet educational leaders.

For inspiration, I acknowledge my third granddaughter, *Yael Avital Macon.* Like her two older sisters, she may now see her name in a book.

ABOUT THE AUTHOR

Mark F. Goldberg, Ph.D., had a thirty-two-year public school career in New York State, including twenty-four years as an administrator on Long Island. For the past twelve years, Goldberg has been an education writer and book editor as well as a consultant and speaker. His publications include four previous books, ninety articles in such educational journals as *Phi Delta Kappan* and *Educational Leadership,* and chapters in two books. Goldberg has worked as both an acquisition and development editor with more than fifty authors and has helped shepherd forty-two books to publication, more than half of them with ASCD and Corwin Press. Goldberg now lives in Austin, Texas, and can be reached at Mark12738@aol.com or by fax at 512-257-7581.

Insider's Guide to School Leadership

Introduction

This book is short and direct. There are no quotations, no footnotes—just highly informed common sense built on more than four decades in education as a teacher, administrator, consultant, education writer, and editor. The "common sense" in this book is strengthened by my twenty-four years as a public school administrator, my visits to excellent schools, and my familiarity with many best practices that have been described in recent articles and books. I neither denigrate nor disregard research and scholarship, but there is simply not enough research on the daily issues that confront assistant principals, department chairs, principals, and curriculum directors to offer you adequate help in meeting the challenges you face as an active school administrator.

There are no absolute answers for how to break up every sort of student fight in a middle school, what to do when your faculty is divided over how best to approach new state standards, or how exactly to work with parents under all sorts of conditions and for different purposes. However, successful and seasoned administrators have developed many techniques that can serve as guidelines.

The caveat here is that nothing will transfer unalloyed from one situation to another. You must always consider your particular skills and inclinations as well as the local circumstances. There is no such thing as a generic leader for all situations. We've all observed a bright, mature, dedicated principal or assistant superintendent succeed in one setting and then not do nearly as well in another school or district, or sometimes simply fail in a setting that is a very poor fit.

In a complex school system such as New York City, with over a million students, what works might be slightly or markedly different from what works in a community with two thousand students in Texas or South Dakota, where there may be less bureaucracy and fewer contractual disputes. Also, the variety of schools and school cultures is far more stunning than it was ten or twenty or thirty years ago. From big-city and suburban high schools with 2,000 or more students and many course offerings and programs to general-purpose minischools at all grade levels with under 250 students and schools with single-theme programs, from charter schools to magnet schools, the variations are endless, as are parental and community demands.

This amazing variety of school cultures and circumstances make generalizations and fiats about administrative behavior or training very difficult. That is why several colleges of education are beginning to train principals for small urban schools or headmasters for private schools or superintendents for large suburban districts, rather than continuing the one-size-fits-all training for every administrative position.

Even within a particular school, there is often no obvious answer to a difficult issue. For instance, it's early spring, and you have to weigh the merits of offering a third year to a teacher under your supervision. That second-year teacher continues to have considerable difficulty with classroom management, but is very strong in her subject, math, and that strength will be hard to replace in your community. Further, she is close to two successful and experienced teachers in the building who have considerable sway with the faculty. Her attitude is excellent, and she frequently volunteers to serve on committees, but you know it will be at least two or three years before she grows into the ability to manage a class with real effectiveness. What do you do? What guidelines might help? How much time will you and others have to help her? Should you recommend renewal for another year, or should you let her go and do the best search you can to find a "better" instructor?

There is no textbook answer. Try Chapter Eight, on supervision, for some "rules" that might help with this and similar situations that present themselves every year to test a supervisor's mettle. Administrators soon learn that much of their work is making mature, considered judgments in situations where there is no inarguably correct answer.

Administrators complain, with justification, that their jobs have become more burdensome in the past twenty-five years. From No Child Left Behind to budget constraints; from state-required drug awareness presentations to violence in schools; from personnel issues to making excellent use of critical thinking, differentiated instruction, and cooperative learning; from textbook selection and staff development to classroom management; from meetings and conferences to required, often complex, forms and new tests—it is the rare administrator who believes he or she has enough time to stay on top of all the new demands, let alone get the daily job done.

This book is divided into eleven chapters, each giving advice or "rules" for how you as administrator might proceed in a way that is concrete, yet leaving room for adjustments to your real situation. The primary readers of this book will be principals, assistant principals, and department or subject-area chairs. Assistant superintendents for instruction and curriculum or personnel will find many useful applications. Teachers who play a role in the governance of their school, who hope to play a governance role, or who aspire to be administrators will find this book useful. (This group grows larger every year as teachers are properly included more and more in decision making and school governance.)

You can select those areas of greatest or immediate interest or read the whole book and then concentrate on areas of personal concern. The order of the chapters is in no way intended to indicate a hierarchy of importance, which will vary from district to district and reader to reader. There certainly is no effort to be comprehensive, although I did try my best to cover many areas of common and significant interest.

In a field as human and variegated as education, a truly comprehensive book cannot exist. This book could have been 100 or 200 or 500 pages longer, and there is room for honest debate about which topics should have been included. My primary consideration was to write a book that would be immediately useful and that most readers would feel addressed several of their most important concerns. My hope is that you will keep this book close by and turn to it for advice dozens of times during the school year.

You may note some redundancy, not more than warranted, as you learn about various aspects of leadership and administration. Some of the skills related to supervision also play a role, for instance, in staff development or running a meeting.

At the end of each chapter, I supply several keywords that will lead you to much more information about the topics covered, and there will also be some overlap from chapter to chapter. Dozens of forms and tables and hundreds of references would have made this book too unwieldy for a guide or handbook. There are many fine articles and books on each of the major topics I cover in this work, and they are easily located on the Internet.

If I've learned anything in more than forty years in education—almost all of it in public education—it is that each school's precise situation is somewhat different from that of its counterparts, even in the same geographical area. Although I supply many real-world examples in this book, the exact details of what can or should be done in a particular school are best left to that school's administrators and staff.

Schools have individual cultures established over many years, and the cultures have many different bases. A school with students from ten or fifteen different ethnic groups may be very different, in fascinating ways, from a school that is more homogeneous. Schools in poor areas often have different challenges and develop a culture different from that of schools in more affluent areas. Some schools are characterized as progressive, whereas others are more conservative as a result of years of local preference—and of course, all the intermediate points between very progressive and extremely conservative are represented in U.S. schools, not to mention that there are outstanding and failing schools in each of the categories.

Giving extremely general advice to administrators is often useless, yet highly specific advice implies that there is but one way to do things. I've tried to furnish "rules" that are grounded in reality and that are meant to be partly broken or stretched or contracted—but not dismissed—to fit authentic circumstances: yours, and those of your place of work. Those rules are buttressed by examples, guidelines, directions, and encouragement that should help any practicing administrator.

Recruitment and Retention

Assuming that you are going to remain in your administrative position for several years, the most important thing you can do is hire excellent people: teachers, custodians, principals, assistant principals, department chairs, school aides, and others with whom you can work well and who will fit the developing view of a culture that you share with your staff or encourage as part of your school's renewal.

These people will likely have considerable allegiance to you because you were instrumental in selecting them. Perhaps of even more importance, over a period of several years, these are the people who will assist you in putting your stamp or notion of culture on the organization, to the reasonable extent that you can and wish to change the organization. No matter who you are, you cannot do anything of significance alone! The days of the powerful leader who dictates policy are over. The job is just too complex for that. Without question, a "strong" leader will always make a difference, but in almost any school organization in the early twenty-first century, it takes a team with many skills to maintain a fine program, renew a school or district, or bring about a serious—let alone seismic—cultural shift.

RULE NUMBER ONE: SET UP A LOGICAL AND EFFECTIVE RECRUITMENT COMMITTEE

If, for example, you are recruiting an English department chairperson, obviously you will want two or three English or humanities teachers on the committee. Just as crucial will be having one teacher from some other discipline, maybe a parent or even a high school student, and one administrator on this committee—perhaps an assistant principal or a chairperson of some other department. You may or may not wish to have the current chairperson of the English department, the person who is leaving, on this committee.

Be sure the English teachers represent different grade levels, somewhat different points of view, and different levels of experience. Don't choose three like-minded "usual suspects," the same teachers who often serve on committees. Of course, you may wish to have some very informal conversations with prospective committee members to make sure they want cultural changes similar to the ones you want. You should tolerate and even promote some differences, but not cultural subversion.

RULE NUMBER TWO: ESTABLISH CLEAR EXPECTATIONS FOR THE NEW POSITION

Just what, precisely, are your expectations and those of the committee for your junior high school's new chief custodian? There are really three serious questions here:

- What are the limitations on the new hire: the civil service list, political considerations, the number of dollars available for the complete salary package? Be coldly realistic.

- What are your, not the committee's, top one or two needs? Make these clear at the outset. Depending on what you need, you may ask the committee to consider your needs seriously as they think about priorities, or you may insist that at least your one top priority be included among the four or five priorities developed by the committee.

- Make the list of expectations manageable and determine which could be negotiable. Having a list of fifteen or twenty expectations is the same as having no list. Crafting a thoughtful list of four to six major or central expectations is very helpful. The expectations should be clear, operational, and available to all candidates before the interview.

  Example of one expectation: as part of a final interview, the two finalists will demonstrate the ability to determine what work needs to be done and in what priority by walking through two classrooms and completing the district work-order form. Each candidate will be provided thirty minutes for this task after having the work-order form carefully explained to him.

RULE NUMBER THREE: CHARGE THE COMMITTEE WITH CREATING AN EVALUATION RUBRIC

Committees don't have unlimited time, so application of the rubric might be restricted to the final two to three candidates. The rubric must be strongly related to the expectations, should have no more than five or six characteristics, and should include either four or five levels of competence.

Here is an example of one item in a rubric for an assistant principal who will play an important role in curriculum in a middle school; it is followed by a list of levels of competence:

Item 1: Demonstrates knowledge of the field by impressive review of state and national requirements; suggests pertinent local issues; is aware of several important issues and concerns that have appeared in the past few years in such publications as *Educational Leadership, Education Week,* and *Phi Delta Kappan.*

Example of Levels of Competence

High competence. Discussed issues easily and knowledgeably; brought up most important issues, including some the committee had not considered; had good understanding of application to local concerns and classroom performance.

Good competence. Discussed most issues easily and relatively thoroughly; needed some prompting on selected issues; had basic understanding of some issues of local concern and classroom performance.

Average competence. Discussed several issues, but occasionally was less than thorough or completely informed; needed a fair amount of prompting to discuss selected issues; not always certain about local and classroom applications.

Below-average competence. Discussed a few issues, mostly superficially; needed considerable prompting to go on; had very limited ability to discuss local concerns or classroom performance.

You will not always be able to locate a candidate with high competence, but you never want to hire below good competence, if that is at all possible. While you are going through the interview process, always keep in mind the possibility of growth. If, for instance, a candidate has taken courses to learn new information, attended conferences at some inconvenience or expense, subscribed to several pertinent journals, or done considerable research to learn about your school and community, those are good signs of a willingness, even an eagerness, to grow. A young or relatively inexperienced candidate who has made this effort but rates only at the bottom of your good category may be an excellent choice.

RULE NUMBER FOUR: RESEARCH THE CANDIDATE COMPLETELY AND EFFECTIVELY

Although you will call back a small number of candidates who do well in the first interview, you have only one opportunity to go through the initial interview process, so you want to learn as much helpful and revealing information about the candidate as the position warrants and is legally permissible. The goal for any new hire is to choose the person about whom you will be just as enthusiastic two years later as you were when you and your committee first made the decision to offer the position to him.

- For a teacher or administrator, ask if the candidate has a portfolio. Portfolios are becoming more common; some colleges even require new teacher graduates to accumulate a portfolio for job interviews.

- A portfolio might include a video of parts of several lessons from student teaching or previous teaching. There are often examples of student work or artifacts related to planning. An administrator's portfolio might include anything from a Friday memo to some material related to budget, supervision, or scheduling. Some administrators submit part of the record of a presentation to their current faculty, administrative council, or board of education.

- References can be laden with traps. Most people can get three or four good references, but those are not always to be fully trusted. Consider the quality of the reference: Did this person see the candidate on the job in the last six months? Is this someone in your local area you can easily contact for more detailed information? Was the reference in a position to supervise the candidate and know this person's work rather well?

- It is a good idea to follow most written references with a phone call. Ask questions about any aspects of the reference that interest or bother you. Always ask, "Is there anything else I should know? Is there any reason you know of why I should be hesitant to hire this person? On a scale of 1 to 10, 10 being the highest, how would you rate this person for the position we have available? Again, is there anything else I should ask or know?"

- If at all possible, visit the one, two, or three finalists at their place of work. Ask if you can be free to ask questions of anyone you wish. The more that is hidden from you or denied to you, the more you should worry. It is important to see several people individually who work directly with the candidate. You are more likely to get some very candid off-the-record comments in a one-to-one setting than in a group where people will worry about confidentiality. These staff members may be concerned about revealing confidential information in a setting where some other group member might reveal what was said at a later time.

- Some schools now routinely do a criminal background check for each finalist. Consult your school attorney and local police to learn what is legal and ethical.

- Virtually every professional position will require several forms of writing: reports to parents, e-mail to staff, a summary of custodial work completed, a brief article for the district newsletter or newspaper, program proposals, and so on. As part of a final interview, it is a very good idea to give finalists an appropriate prompt and ask them to write a short response. The last thing you want is a new teacher, administrator, or chief custodian whose work you must edit heavily or whose work will cause you embarrassment.

Of course, the finalists should know from the get-go that this writing sample will be part of the process, that it will be done as part of a second or third interview and cannot be submitted in advance, and that it will be judged as a first draft. Candidates should be assured that you are not searching for Nobel Prize writing, just writing that is professionally acceptable and that could be improved in a subsequent draft or with very modest help. Your standard for "acceptable" writing will vary by position. The English teacher or principal will be held to a higher standard than the chief custodian whose writing for eyes beyond his or her immediate staff could be edited.

RULE NUMBER FIVE: PROVIDE AN EFFECTIVE MENTOR FOR THE NEW HIRE

Each committee will go through whatever procedures are required in its locality to gain final board approval, but the moment approval is completed, the mentoring program should begin. The mentor is often one person, but there could be more than one person for different purposes.

• Do something more than just make a phone call informing the new hire that she got the job—make her feel welcome and on her way to success. Invite her for a congratulatory visit, which could be anything from a one-hour opportunity to meet a few people, have a cup of coffee, or even an invitation to a formal dinner. This should be followed by one or more "working" visits before the actual date of hire, if this is at all feasible. The mentor will play a leading role in setting up these working visits, making sure the new hire meets as many people who can be of assistance to her when she hits the ground walking fast, not running, on her first day. (There is still more to learn early in a new assignment. "Running" is more likely to lead to tripping!)

• The mentor should not be a person who will evaluate the new hire in any way. The mentor could be a teacher for a new teacher, a chairperson of another department for a new chairperson, and so on, but not someone clearly "above" the new hire in the supervisory hierarchy.

• Work out a method of either giving the mentor time to do this important task or compensating the mentor in some acceptable way (a stipend, funds for conference attendance, or supplies and equipment the mentor would not otherwise get).

• Be clear about the amount of time expected of the mentor. The duration of the role should be at least one year. The weekly or monthly time expectations can vary with need, but there must be a minimum expectation. Many mentors, in my experience, take professional pride in being of help to a new colleague and will voluntarily exceed the minimum expectation.

• Choose a mentor who is not necessarily an expert in every aspect of the new person's job, but can guide the person to people who can help. A new principal may need to find a real estate agent or a pediatrician, and the mentor may wish to suggest several people or recommend a couple of staff members who know more about this than she does. Some schools or districts even have a list of people in various professions whom people new to the community might wish to consult. Larger communities often have some form of newcomer's group.

Rules for Recruitment and Retention

1. Set up a logical and effective recruitment committee.

2. Establish clear expectations for the new position.

3. Charge the committee with creating an evaluation rubric.

4. Research the candidate completely and effectively.

5. Provide an effective mentor for the new hire.

Keywords

Background checks

Building leadership capacity in schools

Hiring teachers

Interview techniques

Mentoring programs for schools

Mentors in schools

Rubrics

Rubrics for schools

School administrator portfolios

Teacher portfolios

Teacher recruitment

Teacher retention

Safety and Emotional Well-Being

Educators at all levels spend most of their time on educational matters, and that is how it should be, even though education is only the *third* priority in a school. Any veteran administrator or teacher knows that physical safety is the first priority and that emotional well-being is the second; then comes education, properly the most time-consuming—but not the highest—priority by far.

Every experienced educator has seen the effect of taunting—including racial, ethnic, and religious taunting—and bullying on students. A few administrators, myself included, have had to call a parent to inform him or her of a serious injury or worse. No administrator can prevent every form of harm all the time, but every administrator must do all in his or her power to ensure that such harm, emotional or physical, occurs as infrequently as possible.

RULE NUMBER ONE: CONDUCT REGULAR INSPECTIONS OF THE SCHOOL

To make certain that all physical safety features are in order, check everything: the eye wash in the chemistry lab in a secondary school, the fire safety doors that open to the outside play areas in an elementary school, and dozens of other items.

- Create a list of the fifty or sixty major safety items. The chief custodian and a representative of the local fire department can help with this.

- Assign someone the responsibility for this inspection: chief custodian, chief custodian and the principal, chief custodian and assistant principal. The responsible party should sign off on this complete inspection at least twice each year. One major inspection should be completed each summer about two weeks before school opens.

- Carefully compile a list of defects and include some indication of the degree of severity, the recommended action, and the date of expected repair. Many schools have very simple (one-page!) work-order forms. Of course, whoever is designated as responsible needs to follow up to make sure such repairs are completed properly and in some reasonable priority order.

RULE NUMBER TWO: MAKE THE SCHOOL AS PERSONAL AS POSSIBLE

In an elementary school, the classroom teacher gets to know students quite well. In secondary schools with more than fifty students per grade, an advisory system is needed to personalize the school. By including all the professionals in the building in such a system (principal, guidance counselor, social worker, librarian, everyone!), most schools will have a ratio of no more than sixteen or seventeen students to one professional—and frequently the number may be even lower.

There are many variations on advisory systems, but they share four characteristics:

- The adviser must have daily contact with each advisee, usually in a group setting similar to traditional homeroom.

- The adviser must meet individually with each student about once each month.

- The adviser should be the person to whom everyone in the school gives important information about his or her advisees.

- The adviser should have contact with parents two to four times each year, by phone or in person.

This system allows the adviser to have a strong relationship with each advisee, to be of help to students, to see the "full picture" of each advisee, and, one hopes, to pick up signs of danger. The system is not perfect, but it's the best one we have and the one most likely to alert the adviser to student problems ranging from poor study habits, homework issues, and minor discipline problems to serious distress that could lead to tragedy.

In a secondary school where classroom teachers see 80 to 150 students each day and guidance counselors commonly have 200 to 500 students in their responsibility, you cannot depend on anyone other than an adviser to ensure that every student is well known to at least one adult. We cannot prevent every Columbine or Red Lake, but an advisory system that personalizes the school and brings every student without exception in close contact with a faculty member will help identify students in distress.

RULE NUMBER THREE: PROTECT STUDENTS FROM INTRUSION AND DISRUPTION

Although several very dramatic and tragic events have occurred in schools in the past fifteen years, most of the evidence is that schools remain extremely safe places. It is also clear, however, that no school—not a rural school, not a city school, not a suburban school—can consider itself exempt from every form of intrusion and disruption. Personalization in the form of small schools or an advisory system will help, but that is just one important part of the answer, and clearly personalization has no effect on intrusion or disruption from outside the school.

Each school needs to exercise control over who enters school property and for what purposes. Some schools need more controls than others, but erring on the side of safety is always a good idea. No one wants a school that operates like an armed camp, but because no school is immune to unwelcome visitors or severely disruptive student behavior, responsible precautions must be taken.

- Form a committee of school personnel and parents who meet at least once each year to talk about physical safety needs.

- Create a clear safety policy. The policy should list the major safety measures that need to be in place, and this must not be a vague list. "A school aide will patrol the school grounds" is far too vague. "One school aide will patrol the perimeter of the school, making a complete circuit at least once every two hours. The precise route and time should be varied and random each day to avoid predictability."

- Consult your local police department for advice on safety measures and policies as well as conditions under which you should call for law enforcement help.

Have in place a realistic policy for how to behave in an emergency. This policy can be crafted with help from the local police and should be reviewed twice each school year. More will be said about this under Rule Number Six.

RULE NUMBER FOUR: CREATE EFFECTIVE SYSTEMS FOR KEEPING TRACK OF STUDENTS

Generally speaking, the culture of a school should be supportive, nurturing, yet educationally demanding. In grades K–12, schools operate *in loco parentis,* which means that the teachers and administrators are responsible, within the bounds of reason and prudence, for knowing where students are at all times and ensuring that they are safe.

When a secondary student is missing (cutting class, not to be found), an effort should be made to find that student, notify the parents or guardians that the student is not where he or she is supposed to be, or both. The system for keeping track of students should be serious and systematic, yet it must not be so unwieldy or demanding that it cannot work. There's no need for an all-out search every time a student is ten minutes late for something or cuts a class, unless this is a known "vulnerable" student (severely learning disabled, prone to violence, and so on). However, if a secondary student is habitually missing for periods of time or is missing for, say, ninety minutes, some serious action is warranted. Obviously, the "allowable" time missing will be much shorter in an elementary school, decreasing to zero for children in the earliest grades.

RULE NUMBER FIVE: PROTECT THE EMOTIONAL WELL-BEING OF STUDENTS

If a student is taunted or bullied for any reason, the student will have a difficult time in school. The advisory system in a secondary school can help, of course, and the school should have a supportive and visible student management program in place that fits the culture of that particular school and that has been the subject of appropriate staff development. Teachers, parents, school aides, administrators, counselors, a social worker, and the school psychologist have roles to play here. In secondary schools, and particularly high schools, students are often included in initial planning or revision of an existing policy.

There are many programs available to help with bullying in the elementary grades or with classroom discipline problems in upper grades.

RULE NUMBER SIX: HAVE AN UP-TO-DATE CRISIS MANAGEMENT BOOKLET AND TEAM

Like a broken record, I repeat that most of the professionals' time in a school will be spent on instruction, curriculum, assessment, staff development, and other important educational activities. However, when you work with hundreds of young people and dozens of adults, sadly but inevitably some very bad things will happen, often outside of school hours. A student will be assaulted, an emergency will be in progress during school hours, a much-loved teacher will die suddenly, a student will die or be badly injured, or some other terrible calamity will occur. Many of these events, obviously, will occur with little or no notice. This is why it is important to put together an emergency or crisis management booklet and continue to revise it as necessary.

Following are some of the things you should consider in creating a crisis management booklet and crisis management team.

- Create a crisis management booklet. If one doesn't exist, it must be started immediately. The central office and probably the board of education will be involved, as well as a representative from each school. There will probably be a district-level master booklet that describes roles for individual schools. Many districts and educational publishers have such documents, so you need never start at square one, although you will have to adjust many of the details to fit your district's needs and preferred responses. The next step is to create the crisis management team.

- Who are the five to seven crisis team members you can call on any time of the day or night? Obviously, an administrator and a "counselor" (guidance counselor, social worker, psychologist) should be team members. The call may come only once in two years, but when it does, the team members must, if at all possible, make themselves immediately available, so except for at least one administrator, clearly this must be a voluntary group and needs to be renewed each year.

- Who will chair this crisis team? More often than not, it should be a very mature and seasoned staff member, usually an administrator, school psychologist, or social worker.

- Who will be the backup person for each team position or role?

- What will be the roles of the various team members, and who will join the team from an individual school, as necessary? This includes one person who gathers accurate information as quickly as possible and remains as the information clearinghouse for the first forty-eight hours or so.

- Who will activate the telephone tree, so that all the people who need to know what happened get the necessary information quickly and accurately?

- Who will be the spokesperson for the team, the one person to whom authorities or members of the media are directed by the other team members?

- Who will lead whatever actions need to be taken during school hours (often the principal, but not necessarily)? There may be situations where the principal is kept informed and takes a secondary role, yielding to a school psychologist, chief custodian, or superintendent of buildings and grounds, depending on the incident.

- Who will put together any grief counseling group or other help group that needs to be constituted?

- Will the school district's attorney need to be involved? At what point and how often? Will the attorney need to be physically present?

- Who will draft, by the second or third day, the accurate and brief narrative of what took place, including problems or issues to be addressed in the future?

- Most crises are negative, as the word suggests. To stretch the word a bit, however, there are occasionally and happily positive crises, such as being named a National Blue Ribbon School or having a student win a major award, such as a high place in the Intel competition. These happy events attract media attention, and your crisis team should be prepared to deal with them as well. It is especially important to have the proper spokesperson and to control the media demands.

- A final caution is that the crisis management team should meet for at least half a day each year, usually very early in the school year, to discuss roles, make changes, and role-play some possible situations.

> **Rules for Safety and Emotional Well-Being**
>
> **1.** Conduct regular inspections of the school.
>
> **2.** Make the school as personal as possible.
>
> **3.** Protect students from intrusion and disruption.
>
> **4.** Create effective systems for keeping track of students.
>
> **5.** Protect the emotional well-being of students.
>
> **6.** Have an up-to-date crisis management booklet and team.

Keywords

Advisory
Advisory programs for schools
Bullying in schools
Classroom management
Crisis management
Crisis management booklet
Crisis management in schools
Crisis management plan for schools
Crisis management team
Discipline programs
Emergency management in schools
Emotional intelligence
Fire safety in schools
School crisis management
School programs for bullying
School safety
School safety list
Schools and police

Keeping Up

Administrative practices, laws, and teaching methods are changing rapidly in education. New state and federal laws, revised regulations and methods of assessment, what is known about how children learn—these are but a small portion of the changes. Even if we were to do nothing else, none of us could stay on top of more than a few of the developments across all the disciplines and grades.

RULE NUMBER ONE: MAINTAIN A HIGH STANDARD OF KNOWLEDGE IN THE PROFESSION

Everyone has to make choices about how to stay abreast of developments, so every educator should belong to one or two relevant national professional organizations. If, for example, you are the English department chairperson, you will probably join the National Council of Teachers of English. Many principals join the National Association of Elementary School Principals or the National Association of Secondary School Principals.

There are several excellent organizations that cut across disciplines. The Association for Supervision and Curriculum Development (ASCD) covers just about any development in education. Its main journal, *Educational Leadership,* does theme issues, covering such topics as reading, special education, and testing. The National Staff Development Council and the American Educational Research Association (AERA) are two other organizations with appeal across disciplines, grades, and issues. Certainly Phi Delta Kappa (PDK), the professional association for educators, and its journal the *Kappan* are important.

Education Week is the quality newspaper of the education profession. It includes dozens of topical articles, commentary and editorials, lists of conferences, summaries of important statistical information, and other features of great value to educators. This is the single best way to maintain contact with the profession as a whole, although the publications referred to earlier are superior for curricular and subject-area information as well as carefully developed articles on everything from testing to class size.

RULE NUMBER TWO: FOLLOW A SMALL SELECTION OF SPECIAL INTERESTS

In addition to maintaining a general knowledge of important developments, follow with care just two or three areas of special interest. The English chairperson who has a special interest in writing might join the National Writing Project and follow developments through that organization. ASCD has special-interest groups that have newsletters and meet at their annual national conference. If you have a deep interest in assessment, AERA is a good match and can lead you to areas of special interest.

RULE NUMBER THREE: TAKE ADVANTAGE OF THE RESOURCES IN YOUR AREA

• Form a small learning community. There are probably other professionals in your building or district with similar interests. You can meet during the school day or outside of school hours to talk about what you're learning—developments in science, initial reading, scheduling, standards, or classroom management. You can make synergistic use of the group by occasionally reading different things and sharing what you've learned. Members of the group might even agree to belong to different professional organizations, making it possible to share journals, newsletters, and other materials.

• Learn what professional groups exist in your city, region, county, or state. See what resources your state education department or area group has to offer. Many of the national educational organizations, such as PDK or the ASCD, have local or state chapters. Many subject-area groups have local or state organizations, and most states have professional organizations for administrators, usually divided by elementary and secondary. For administrators at any level, colleagues in nearby schools or districts facing problems similar to yours can be of inestimable value.

• Take advantage of expertise in your school district. Some of the parents may be psychologists, mathematicians, contractors, supervisors, writers, educators, police or fire personnel, small business owners . . . Find out what special skills they possess and might be willing to offer your learning group. From advice on dealing with school safety to getting the best prices for small repairs, from looking at new math materials to giving help with some administrative management issues, parents can be great resources and almost never ask for payment. Perhaps two or three of your learning community's meetings each year could even include a parent guest or panel.

RULE NUMBER FOUR: REVIEW RECENT DEVELOPMENTS IN EDUCATION

Think of these terms as additional keywords. They are accompanied by some guiding information intended to suggest what these topics include rather than serve as definitions.

If a topic you think is very important is not on this list, please remember that I or any other experienced educator could have made this list ten or even twenty-five or more items longer. I tried to pick issues that many veteran educators would agree were of importance, whether for their intrinsic value or because of mandates.

Accountability   Includes standards, all forms of assessment to measure achievement of standards, and any regulations in your state that govern standards and assessment

Achievement gap   Usually refers to the gap between test scores achieved by high-achieving students and those of students who struggle on standardized tests, often poor or minority students

Advanced Placement (AP) and other advanced courses   Refers to AP, International Baccalaureate (IB) programs, and any other programs taken by high-achieving secondary students, often to gain college credit or prestige

Advisory system   Refers to any of the variations on programs designed to personalize the school to the point where at least one adult has a close relationship with each student

Attention deficit disorder   Refers to students who have serious difficulty staying on task for any reason

Authentic assessment   Includes all forms of performance assessment and real-world assessment, as opposed to such methods as multiple choice, short answer, and other easily scored paper-and-pencil tests

Bilingual education   Includes both traditional bilingual education and some of the more recent programs that insist on students' being immersed in English very quickly and moved to all-English programs in six to eighteen months

Brain-based teaching   Includes all of the practical work based on sound research that helps teachers understand how to make use of what we know about learning and about how the brain develops and works

Character education   Refers to programs that include the learning of strong ethical and moral values as an important component of education

Constructivism   Refers to methods that emphasize experiential learning and especially the learning of concepts or possible solutions to problems by exploring and working through the problems

Core knowledge   Relates to the work of E. D. Hirsch Jr. and emphasizes mastering a body of knowledge as the foundation for mastering more knowledge and then concepts; most of this work relates to elementary grades

Differentiated instruction   Refers to all programs that vary instruction by student or small-group need

Disaggregation of data   Refers to presenting test results broken out by subgroups, such as boys and girls, minority students, or students with disabilities

Essential questions   Refers to an approach in which instructional units are organized around broad-based questions on important themes

Governance structure   Refers to how decisions are made in a school or school district, but often also to structures that to some extent decentralize or rearrange the traditional hierarchy

High-stakes tests   Refers to all tests that place students at risk of not moving up to the next grade or that must be "passed" in order for the student to exit some phase of education, such as high school

Individuals with Disabilities Education Act (IDEA)   The federal law that governs how students with disabilities must be treated

Multicultural education   Includes any programs that celebrate diversity and include learning about the many cultures in our society

Multiple intelligences (MI)   Refers to the work originally done by Professor Howard Gardner of Harvard and the many subsequent programs that emphasize the idea of a range of intelligences, not just cognitive intelligence, as well as the books and materials available that provide MI classroom activities

No Child Left Behind (NCLB)   The federal law that regulates how schools must achieve; it has undergone some changes in interpretation and likely will continue to undergo change, including change in the law itself in 2007, when the law is due for review

Portfolios   Includes any system by which students collect work in a portfolio for evaluation; there are also teacher and administrator portfolios

Problem-based learning   Refers to an approach in which students or professional study groups are presented with a "messy" problem that has no one correct answer and must devise ways to "solve" the problem, almost always working in small groups

Rubric   Refers to any assessment that describes to students or others the characteristics of success as well as the criteria for determining the degree of success

Untracking   Refers to any program that emphasizes mixed-ability grouping over grouping by ability

World-class standards   Refers to any program that sets the bar high enough to train students to be competitive with the highest-achieving students in other highly industrialized nations

---

Rules for Keeping Up

1. Maintain a high standard of knowledge in the profession.

2. Follow a small selection of special interests.

3. Take advantage of the resources in your area.

4. Review recent developments in education.

Keywords

Accountability in education
Achievement gap
Advanced Placement (AP)

Advisory system in education

American Association of Physics Teachers (AAPT)

American Association of School Administrators (AASA)

American Council on the Teaching of Foreign Languages (ACTFL)

Association for Supervision and Curriculum Development (ASCD)

Attention deficit disorder

Authentic assessment

Brain-based education

Character education

Coalition of Essential Schools (CES)

Constructivism

Core Knowledge Foundation

Differentiated instruction

Educational Leadership

Education Week

Essential questions

Governance structure: Education

Heterogeneous classes

High-stakes tests

Individuals with Disabilities Education Act (IDEA)

International Reading Association (IRA)

Learning communities

Multicultural education

Multiple intelligences (MI)

National Art Education Association (NAEA)

National Association of Biology Teachers (NABT)

National Association of Elementary School Principals (NAESP)

National Association of Secondary School Principals (NASSP)

National Council for the Social Studies (NCSS)

National Council of Teachers of English (NCTE)

National Council of Teachers of Mathematics (NCTM)

National Science Teachers Association (NSTA)

National Staff Development Council (NSDC)

National Writing Project (NWP)

No Child Left Behind (NCLB)

Phi Delta Kappa (PDK)

Phi Delta Kappan

Portfolios

Problem-based learning

Rubrics in education

Study groups

Untracking

World-class standards

chapter FOUR

Meetings

I f you are in any type of supervisory position, you will need to call meetings from time to time to discuss important issues. The general rules of thumb are few and simple:

- Call only meetings that are genuinely important both to you and the group.
- Always have an agenda.
- Keep the meetings as focused and as short as possible. This does not mean that every meeting should be a maximum of thirty minutes—some meetings may warrant an hour or two or even longer for a very controversial, complex, or difficult issue.

Simply put, meetings should not go beyond the point of productivity or tolerance. The longer the meeting, the more the need for an occasional break of five to ten minutes during which people can stretch, leave the room, socialize, or even discuss the issue at hand in a more relaxed way. Any meeting that lasts one hour or more should include some modest refreshments if at all possible.

RULE NUMBER ONE: SCHEDULE MEETINGS ONLY WHEN TRULY NECESSARY AND PREPARE FOR THEM CAREFULLY

Let's suppose that you are an elementary school principal and are having some problems with the schedule and content coordination of the science person who teaches every Tuesday and Friday in your building.

- Always ask yourself first, "Do I really need a meeting to solve this problem?" Before scheduling a meeting, make certain that you can't get the information you need from the teachers via e-mail (fairly quickly and easily) and resolve the problem with the science specialist yourself.

• If you do need a meeting, be sure the right people are present to solve the problem. In our example, is a meeting of all the elementary teachers with the science person the answer? Perhaps a smaller group could meet—say, just the fifth-grade teachers—and solutions derived from that meeting could be used to help with other grades. Grade representatives might be another possibility. The bottom line: everyone at the meeting should have a stake in the outcome and should potentially have something to contribute.

• Schedule the meeting at a time reasonably convenient for all parties and state what needs to be solved or resolved. Remember, the people you invite are just as busy as you are, and their time is just as important to them.

• Create a very specific agenda. The agenda is very important, even crucial. It is a mistake to say, "We're meeting to figure out how better to use the science coordinator." A more productive approach, for just that one agenda item, might be as follows:

To: Science Coordinating Committee
Fr: Principal
Re: Agenda item 2 for resolution

Sometimes, due to illness, weather, or a school event, the science specialist misses a day with a class. Several teachers have complained that they might be in the middle of an important science unit and it just gets dropped for a week or longer.

Ms. Jones (science specialist) has agreed to submit two short written suggestions that might solve this problem, and I'll get these to you before we meet. I invite any teacher on the science coordination committee to submit a possible solution before the meeting. If I receive these suggestions by Thursday, I'll circulate them before the meeting. Please talk to each other about this in the next few days before we meet next Thursday at 11 A.M.

• Limit the length of the agenda. Most agendas for a short meeting (thirty to sixty minutes) contain no more than three items, and often only one. When there is only one agenda item, that item may be complex or may require considerable discussion.

In the case of the science teacher, keep the first agenda item very simple (perhaps requiring five minutes), then devote the remainder of the meeting to the issue of missed classes.

RULE NUMBER TWO: MAKE MEETINGS WORTHWHILE

Faculty meetings are often the butt of jokes in schools. Too often, they become the principal's meeting or the department chairperson's meeting. Some teachers fail to attend or attend under duress; people read, talk, knit, or otherwise distract themselves from the tedium of the meetings, which often include announcements, minilectures, and nonproductive griping or grandstanding.

Meetings, and especially the many department and faculty meetings that are often regarded as wasted time, should be interesting, useful, solution-oriented, and seen by the staff as worthwhile. They are actually important opportunities for learning and sharing. The hope is that experienced teachers will come to say, "Faculty meetings used to be totally stupid and boring, but now I look forward to them."

As discussed in Rule Number One, preparation is critical to the effectiveness and value of meetings. Do not make the mistake of saying to the thirty, forty, or fifty or more faculty members, "What should we do?" That just leads to the usual gripe session during which people express the same positions they've held for years. Following are some guidelines and possibilities to help you in preparing for meetings:

• The person responsible for the meeting should prepare an agenda, either by himself or, preferably, with one or two other staff members. This agenda should focus on one to three items of importance to most of the people in the group. For instance, if discipline—usually an emotional issue in a school—needs to be discussed by the faculty or some subgroup of the faculty, make it the only agenda item.

• Bring together a small but genuinely representative committee to write a short statement of the discipline issue, to present the issues that vex many faculty members, and, perhaps, to suggest three or four possible ways to resolve the issue. This material should not exceed two pages and should be circulated a week before the full faculty meeting.

• Invite individual faculty members or groups to submit alternative solutions to the problem or to fine-tune solutions that have been proposed. If possible, circulate these possible solutions at least a few days before the meeting to get people talking about the upcoming issue. Make clear that given the opportunities everyone has to prepare for the meeting, the meeting itself is not the time and place to go back to square one.

If you have followed these preparation guidelines, you will be able to begin the faculty meeting much further along, avoiding the problem of those few obstructionists who love to say, "Let's go back to . . ."

• Limit the number of announcements or eliminate them altogether. Announcements are better communicated by e-mail, a Friday memo, or some other technique.

• Divide into work groups of no more than seven people each to take up one possible resolution. People may wish to choose their group by resolution, or you can just count off to form groups. There could be more than one group working on the same resolution.

Each group is obliged to consider and discuss the proposed resolution for forty minutes and then to submit very briefly in writing either the group's refinement of the proposed resolution or a clear statement of why that proposal won't work and, if possible, a description of a solution that might work. All the possible solutions will be circulated to the faculty a day or two after the meeting.

After the meeting, the written material then goes to the small committee that framed the faculty meeting. The committee may arrive at a solution based on the material received, or it may winnow the material down to two possible resolutions that will be submitted to a slightly larger committee or the entire faculty for final resolution or a vote.

Don't worry if you cannot get every faculty member to agree on a solution to a complex or emotionally charged issue. Just make sure you have gone through a fair process and have a strong majority, say 70 percent, behind you. Waiting for 80 percent or more is often tantamount to getting nothing done.

RULE NUMBER THREE: MAKE FACULTY AND DEPARTMENT MEETINGS INTERESTING

• Perhaps there is some adult in your community who can represent a minority group in your school you do not know enough about. A Muslim or Mexican or Jewish or Chinese representative could speak about some of his or her group's sensitivities, perceptions of school, and other issues of great interest to the faculty.

• Consider a faculty meeting where, again dividing into groups, each group reads a short article on a topic of current interest or contention in your school and reports back to the whole faculty on that article and its implications for the school. Groups can read different articles on a theme—say, reading or discipline or technology—or each group can read the same article. Obviously, the subcommittee that chooses the publication(s) should work to find recent articles of unusually high interest for its school.

• Sometimes there are issues around testing or test preparation or some major change that has been imposed on the school due to budget cuts or to a state or federal mandate that "force" the principal or chairperson to use a meeting for a particular concern. Even in these situations, inviting a board member or central office administrator to help explain the issue and using small groups to determine how the faculty can best deal with the issue are far better approaches than simply having the principal or assistant principal make a presentation followed by a nonproductive session of, mostly, griping.

RULE NUMBER FOUR: HOLD A RETREAT FOR MAJOR ISSUES

Group retreats are a great way to build team skills and make accelerated progress on specific issues. They have at least two common characteristics:

• A group of professionals meets in a setting different from and more comfortable than the one in which they usually meet. You may not be able to take your third-grade teachers or administrative staff to an elegant resort, but you should try to find a setting that is pleasant and unusual. This can be the room in which the board meets or some meeting space a local business donates.

• The total time for a retreat is expanded considerably beyond usual meeting times; they often last from a half day to two days.

The subject of the retreat should be a shared issue or two of major import to the school or district, although occasionally a retreat can be held on an issue of great importance to a particular administrator who needs advice and help with a problem. The need for a retreat usually grows out of a gathering frustration over a serious problem or issue that is too large and contentious to resolve in the context of busy school responsibilities.

Examples of Retreat Topics

There have been too many conflicts among the administrators over who, exactly, is responsible for what. A group of four administrators has met once each week for the past six weeks during their common lunch to talk about this. They have identified nine touchy areas where there is overlap and disagreement and have recommended a one-day Saturday retreat to consider these areas and put together a guide not to exceed three pages that will summarize agreements about who has primary responsibility for certain issues. They have also recommended that the guide be reconsidered at an in-school meeting six months hence to see if it is working well.

The board or the superintendent has set a goal for a principal. The principal in turn wishes to share the goal to determine how with staff help she or he can meet the standard that has been set. This might require a half-day retreat with the nine staff members affected by this goal.

A group of six teachers, one assistant principal, and five parents has met four times in the past two months. Some conflict has developed over how final decisions are made. The principal has arranged for the group to meet for a full day to discuss the three methods group members have suggested for resolution.

The retreat is also often a time when people can have an extended lunch together or just take a walk. Some retreats include time for people to talk about themselves and their families or special interests. Although we live in a time of data, more data, and still more data, not to mention the accompanying pressure of tests, it is important to understand that we are nevertheless talking about interesting people of goodwill and honorable intentions working together. Education is a labor-intensive occupation, and the secretaries, custodians, teachers, aides, administrators, and others who work together in a school need to be a well-functioning team.

As we discussed in the case of meetings, preparation is essential to the success of a retreat. Do not underestimate the work it will take before the retreat to create the agenda and make the necessary mundane arrangements; typically, more than one person works on the various tasks involved.

- Assign someone the responsibility for gathering all the materials and making all the arrangements so that routine matters don't get in the way. I've been on too many retreats where someone says, "Well, does anyone have a copy of the test?" or "Did anyone bring eight copies of the student handbook?" or "Is there a computer or calculator we can use?"

- Build an agenda that is clear, that represents the interests of the group, that is modest enough for thorough consideration in the time allotted, and that has a stated general outcome, such as the selection of a new reading series or some workable conclusion on the distribution of major administrative responsibilities among the high school's leadership team.

- Create a schedule with the proper balance of working and nonworking periods. Although retreats promote some socializing and sometimes allow for relaxed meals and other nonworking activities, the working portion needs to be focused and rigorous—it also must occupy by far the majority of time allotted for the retreat.

Now that the planning for the retreat is finished, you need to consider the retreat itself.

- A major mistake at a retreat is to allow it to descend into either a period of unrelieved socializing or a time for endless bickering. Someone must serve as the chair, the person who says lunch is over and who keeps the group focused on the task(s). This person is typically part of the group that planned the retreat. She must be intimately familiar with the agenda and the general goals for the retreat as well as someone held in high regard.

- In those rare instances where the subject of the retreat is extremely volatile and the retreat chair sees a strong possibility of stalemate or worse, it is wise to use an objective facilitator. This can be a paid professional or someone from within the district who does not have a stake in the outcome and is known to have excellent skills for working with groups. This "outside" facilitator needs to be briefed thoroughly on the subject of the retreat well before the meeting, and all parties need to agree that the facilitator will be the "authority" *pro tem* for the retreat.

- A retreat should have an outcome, and all the participants should know before the retreat begins that an outcome is the goal. In the administrative conflict example, the outcome might be a short guide, perhaps three or four pages, describing each role and its major responsibilities. The purpose of the retreat is to create the content of that guide.

The retreat leader(s) should have a plan for how the group will achieve this outcome. This might include discussion, breaking into small groups, starting with items where agreement may be easy to reach and working toward harder issues after the group has had success, and voting after discussion, perhaps even agreeing that an item needs a two-thirds vote to pass.

• The last hour or two of the retreat should be devoted to the outcome. The result need not be a formal written document, although that is helpful. It can be as simple as minutes that contain one or two agreements, a summary of progress made on one difficult item about which no final agreement was reached, or an outline of precisely how and when the final item will be resolved, if that is necessary. The cardinal sin is leaving a retreat in disarray with the feeling that nothing has been accomplished.

RULE NUMBER FIVE: USE FORCED CHOICE AS A LAST RESORT

There are times when groups face issues that are very contentious and messy, that have neither an obvious nor clear answer, and that cannot be resolved by the faculty or a group, even on a retreat. These situations will be very rare—all other options should be tried first—but in the end there can be a Forced Choice solution. I hesitate to give a specific example here, and hope that Forced Choice is a final resort that you exercise only once in two or three years. For obvious reasons, I have saved this option for the end of the chapter.

Let us suppose you have tried to resolve an issue over a period of time, and nothing has worked. The faculty must reach a conclusion within a few weeks on a new reading program, the use of some space, a classroom management approach, or . . . Feelings are running high. At the faculty meeting, you are going to use Forced Choice. Be sure to inform the group or faculty beforehand that a method to reach a decision will be used at this meeting.

• Invite people to form groups around the four choices, discuss the strong points of each choice, and put together a four- or five-sentence argument in favor of each choice.
• List the choices in no particular order and have the faculty rank each choice 1, 2, 3, and 4 (1 being the voter's first choice). The vote should be on a form prepared for the meeting, so people can easily indicate where they stand.

In this example, which for illustration uses only three votes, the faculty are choosing among four reading programs.

Program A: 4, 3, 2 = 9

Program B: 1, 4, 4 = 9

Program C: 3, 2, 3 = 8

Program D: 2, 1, 1 = 4

Because it received the greatest number of high ratings, Program D is the winner. Remember, the lowest number is the winner.

• Put the results of the vote on the board for all to see. Either two or three programs are eliminated by adding up the scores. Generally this works very well, and the winner emerges after one round.

• If after two voting rounds, two options are in a dead heat, a committee with an odd number of people on it, usually five or seven, meets to settle the issue within a few days after the faculty meeting. It is very important that this committee be established and announced before the Forced Choice meeting takes place. The committee members should, to the extent possible, reflect several points of view. The staff members on the committee should be people who are very mature and known to the faculty as fair. The vote of the committee is final after the unsuccessful effort at the larger meeting.

Rules for Meetings

1. Schedule meetings only when truly necessary and prepare for them carefully.

2. Make meetings worthwhile.

3. Make faculty and department meetings interesting.

4. Hold a retreat for major issues.

5. Use Forced Choice as a last resort.

Keywords

Cooperative learning

Department meetings

Educational outcomes

Faculty meetings

Forced Choice

Groups

Learning groups

Staff Development

S taff development, also often called professional development or in-service education, takes many forms: traditional classes, cooperative classes, learning communities, study groups, and other efforts that are under the sponsorship of the school or district and include several, many, or all staff members.

Staff development is absolutely central to having an excellent school and school district. Teachers and administrators will, of course, take college courses of their choice outside the school, and that is good. Sometimes they will even participate in a summer institute or other professional development course or activity that is for their individual growth—also good. However, if you wish to have one or several learning communities in your school to ensure continual teacher growth and professional interaction, if you need to solve individual school problems through study groups, or if you wish to target one or two areas for all or some segment of your staff to study or master, careful and focused professional development is the only road to take.

I can't know how staff development is organized in a particular school district—by subdivisions of a very large district, by individual school, or by some combination of ways. But in this chapter I will assume (hope!) that any organizing entity uses a committee of at least teachers and administrators to set priorities after considered discussion and at the outer limits of a district's financial ability to support staff development—usually priorities that will last one or several years.

Administrators have at least three major responsibilities in staff development:

• They must encourage this form of learning and problem solving, particularly when the staff development meshes with school or district priorities.

- They should take the initiative in suggesting proposals or quickly join groups that are presenting proposals, not necessarily as the group's leader or chair but as one member who can lend powerful support should the proposal turn out to be acceptable. The administrator need not always be a permanent member, but should join for a time, or visit planning groups early in their work.

- They hold the ultimate responsibility for maintaining very high quality in-service instruction in a school or district.

RULE NUMBER ONE: FORM A LEARNING COMMUNITY OR STUDY GROUP

The term *learning community* is used so often and variously that it is in danger of losing any clear meaning. There remain two common characteristics of all learning communities:

- A group of professionals, often dominated by teachers, gathers to approach a problem or issue important to the well-being or academic progress of the school.

- The group studies that problem in a very serious way in the hope of developing recommendations or of finding some practical solutions and curriculum activities that will improve the situation.

The basic idea of a learning community is that we are in this together; no administrator-mandated or other top-down methods are likely to work, at least not without broad approval and enthusiasm, so we must marshal all of our appropriate professional human resources to solve complex problems in schools. Learning communities may use study groups, action groups, problem-based learning, or more traditional professional development courses to help with their work.

- A learning community can last six weeks or six months, depending on the complexity of the problem. Study groups are usually miniature learning communities and will be discussed a bit later in this chapter. If at all possible, an appropriate administrator should be a member of these groups or at least attend as often as possible.

- Learning communities can comprise the entire professional staff of a school, although most often they include some segment of the school, six to as many as fifteen staff members.

- Study groups are often small—four to eight staff members—who focus on an issue of concern to some element of the school's staff: teachers in grades 1 and 2, English teachers, cocurricular advisers, and so on. The group might investigate which new methods for teaching math to upper elementary students would best fit their school, or they might look at three or four math books that are candidates for use in their district or school. The study group makes recommendations or fixes on some new method that draws from several books and other sources. Sometimes the study group continues its work or is followed by much more focused study by a learning community, or by training in a professional development course. Again, some appropriate administrator should join this effort if possible.

- If you are in a school where staff members are not used to taking the initiative in suggesting possible changes, encourage teachers and other staff members to approach you, the administrator, when they wish to suggest some issue for study. For example, perhaps there has been little agreement on an approach to discipline that brings a degree of flexibility to the issue or that leads to some set of discipline guidelines that allow parents, teachers, administrators, and students to understand what is expected and what role each will play.

- Ideas for traditional staff development, usually a course that meets for fifteen to forty-five hours, can come from any group with a stake in the school: parents, administrators, teachers, school aides, even students—or any combination of stakeholders. When the idea comes from you as administrator, you should quickly enlist other staff members in the initial discussion to broaden interest and to make the staff base more inclusive.

The first step toward staff development is to ask the group that suggested the issue to state the problem very clearly in writing. The group should present a brief outline of what they wish to learn or accomplish and an estimate of the time and expense that will be required.

The next step is to work with the teachers, administrators, or others who proposed the study to make certain that it is grounded in reality and is likely to lead to a realistic outcome—perhaps not exactly the outcome you envisioned or even the broad outcome the teachers envisioned at the outset—but a respectable and responsible outcome that grew out of serious study.

RULE NUMBER TWO: BE CERTAIN THAT YOUR STAFF DEVELOPMENT COURSE IS INCLUSIVE AND COMPLETE

• Don't let the usual in-group in the school control the process. A study group's conclusions need to be accepted by the broadest possible audience—not necessarily the entire staff, but typically by 70 percent or so of the group that will consider the study group's recommendations. You won't achieve that level of acceptance if only the "usual suspects" are in the group.

• Be certain that all the players needed to carry out this project are in the group. If you have a serious third-grade teacher who knows a lot about reading or mathematics or differentiated instruction (or whatever the issue is) but was not included in the original group, you need to take that up with the group and encourage them to include that teacher, if not as a member at least as an important "consultant" to the group.

• Size matters. For issues that require a resolution, study groups are a good method. If the group is to take up a focused problem and put together a recommendation or two within eight weeks, it should be small: five to eight people who have appropriate skills for the problem or have a deep interest in the issue at hand. This is not an in-service course, which could be larger, nor is it an effort to turn the whole school or some large segment of the school into a learning community—a good idea but far more complex than a study group.

RULE NUMBER THREE: FOCUS THE STUDY GROUP ON A MANAGEABLE GOAL

Don't give a small study group more than it can handle within the constraints of time and allotted resources. Your school is neither a university nor a research organization. A study group is not an effort to set up control and experimental groups for a serious research study. Other people have already done that. You are perhaps looking at three reading series that might fit your school's needs, investigating two well-known science programs, or considering two or three classroom management systems that seem to fit your school's culture and might improve discipline in your school.

Let's use the example of the review of a new reading series. After the committee has carefully reviewed the three competing reading series, they might contact the publishers' representatives once again to clear up some new questions that have developed. Each member of the committee might be assigned to read one or two articles that describe the approach under consideration, and perhaps two teachers could attend a state conference on reading where a number of people will be present who know about these three candidates for adoption. Two other teachers will visit nearby districts that have adopted each of these series to learn about the advantages and disadvantages the staff has discovered. After telephoning a couple of reading experts and reading a few items on the Internet, the committee should have enough information to enable a clear majority to make a recommendation.

RULE NUMBER FOUR: MAKE STAFF DEVELOPMENT COURSES RELEVANT

Most traditional staff development courses, unless mandated by an outside agency that has clear authority over your work, should be on topics many staff members consider useful.

• Again, suggestions can come from any of the usual school sources: parents, teachers, school aides, classroom volunteers, and administrators. The two critical components for consideration are that there is an audience for the course and a real need for the course. Many schools require a specified minimum number of staff members in order to offer a course.

• Be certain that the in-service class is not hijacked by the usual suspects. Broaden as much as possible the leadership and participation in every phase, from the proposal to the actual course.

• Determine at the outset if the course is one that you wish all teachers to take, perhaps over a period of two or three years; alternatively, it may be important to cycle everyone through during the first year; or, perhaps, this is a course that only a portion of the staff needs to take.

For instance, you can cycle teachers through a National Writing Project (NWP) course over a period of time as long as two or three years, starting with those staff members most eager to learn NWP techniques. All the teachers not in the course will continue to teach composition as they have until they take the course, although invariably they will pick up some techniques from the early attendants in the NWP class.

In contrast, if you are starting an advisory program in a middle school that has never had one, you cannot say to any group of teachers, "Look, do your best with this even though you know almost nothing about it. We'll get to you next year or the year after." You need to train the entire staff to some extent before you begin the advisory program.

• Most professional development courses have appeal only to a portion of the faculty. A course in new materials to use with beginning or severely struggling readers would probably not interest teachers after grade 3, where different approaches might be required. In most secondary schools, professional development in new curriculum materials will apply to subject teachers, but only in their particular area (or areas if they are team-teaching).

RULE NUMBER FIVE: CAREFULLY PLAN AND EXECUTE IN-SERVICE AND PROFESSIONAL DEVELOPMENT COURSES

Most school districts have a limited budget as well as limited time for staff development, and there are usually more traditional courses than study groups or learning communities, although that is changing in some places. Everything I say about high standards and rigor in this rule applies, of course, to all forms of staff development.

• Far too many professional development courses have a reputation for being "soft" or "light" or "loose." That is unacceptable in a school world that is becoming more complex, more demanding, and increasingly in need of highly qualified educators. Of course, the community outside of the school is also asking questions about staff development and voicing demands for rigor.

• Every staff development course should have a chairperson who takes care of such details as scheduling, room arrangements, e-mail announcements, and preparation or collection of materials.

• The committee or the person or people who arrange for the instruction should think hard and worry about the quality of the instruction. If the instructor is an outside expert, several people should have seen this person teach or present at a conference and be convinced that she is good.

• If the instructor or instructors are staff members, or if the course is one that will have shared responsibility, worry about whether the instructors are people with the expertise and appeal to work well with staff. I have seen many outstanding teachers of K–12 students who are not nearly as gifted with adults.

- The professional development class should meet regularly and predictably. Attendance should be taken, and some absolute minimum number of hours must be required for payment or credit. If the course meets for fifteen two-hour sessions (thirty hours), a minimum of twenty-six hours might be required. Keep the minimum high and have some arrangement for makeup of the two sessions missed. Worry continually about rigor and reputation!

- The course should have an outline, and there should be an agenda for each class. Attending staff members should read articles and prepare materials in advance as well as prepare appropriate classroom materials and activities during the class. The course should be focused and demanding. Within the constraints of good sense and any contractual or other agreements in your school district, professional development courses should maintain a reputation for rigor and applicability to real and urgent school issues.

RULE NUMBER SIX: LIMIT THE NUMBER OF PROFESSIONAL DEVELOPMENT CLASSES

In many schools or districts, the limited budget takes care of this rule. The point I wish to make is that you do not want to dilute your priorities. If your current priorities are an advisory system in the high school, more materials for struggling readers in grades 1–3, and infusing more and better science instruction in grades K-6, your professional development should focus on those areas.

Please note that the preceding paragraph makes no mention of priorities for grades 7 and 8 in this particular year. That absence may be a result of your having just spent two years on professional development for advisory in those grades, or it may be that they will be favored in a subsequent year. The implication here is that the district has a multiyear plan for priorities and staff development, subject to some typically minor revision in the light of changing circumstances each year.

More and more school districts, for purposes of coordination and budget, have district priorities. Of course, an individual school may have an additional modest budget for staff development and could mount something needed just in that school in a given year. This should probably be a topic that the staff considers of some urgency for their particular school and that does not conflict with the district's priorities. Examples might be a scheduling inequity or a minor problem with a new reading or math series that could be solved by a short staff development course or a study group.

The amount of time, money, and effort devoted to study groups, learning communities, and courses should vary. Use the method that is most appropriate to the need and assign the time and resources that are likely to get the job done. Don't fall into the trap of making all forms of professional study worth thirty or forty-five hours.

More is said about priorities in Chapter Six.

RULE NUMBER SEVEN: COMPENSATE EVERY GROUP AND COURSE PARTICIPANT

• Many school districts cover compensation in a contract or agreement of some sort. The more limited the words "reward" and "compensation" are, the harder it is to mount in-service programs.

For instance, a group of seven teachers who work in a study group for forty or fifty hours might be willing to accept that over three years, each teacher would be given two days at full pay and up to $600 for expenses to attend an educational conference, with no more than three teachers going in any year.

• Administrators or a negotiating committee might wish to meet with some designated group of staff members to determine what forms of compensation other than outright payment could be agreeable. Paid conference attendance, in-service credit toward salary, additional funds for the purchase of classroom materials for several teachers, materials and equipment to support one teacher's work, and other possibilities have worked in districts around the country.

• Some of the rewards for participating in staff development should be immediate. Certainly businesses understand this, and it is no less important in education. Staff development should be held in the most pleasant and appropriate space available: the board of education meeting room or another suitable meeting room. Some school districts have been able to arrange to use the meeting space in a nearby business building. Meeting from 4 P.M. to 6 P.M. in a classroom not especially appropriate for eighteen adults and not even cleaned yet that day is far from the most inspiring setting for serious learning and discussion. Of course, if you need science labs or other special equipment, you may not be able to get around using a classroom with the required equipment. Whatever materials and equipment will be needed should be supplied and at hand (within reason, depending on the particular school district).

Cold and hot drinks and light refreshments should be available. Everyone knows this, and it is common practice in business, but often it is forgotten, seen as an unnecessary fringe benefit or regarded as politically difficult when many districts are struggling with budget. It's important, it's morale boosting, and it's the adult thing to do!

• Every district has some budget for staff development, however modest. Of course, there are grants, donations (both dollars and in kind), and presentations by vendors. My bias here is clear and strong. I encourage each school district to go as far as it possibly can in providing funds, encouragement, time, supplies, and materials for staff development. This is your investment in your staff; it is your way to increase their skills, and, arguably, it is one of the most powerful ways to increase staff morale, not to be underestimated in a climate where teachers and administrators are under considerable pressure to meet federal and state requirements and in a profession where 45 percent of the people who enter the profession leave within five years.

From the "selfish" perspective of the board and administration, staff development is the way in which you get staff members to engage in common study around issues of importance to you. When these issues merge with the staff's interests, well, that's the ideal.

Rules for Staff Development

1. Form a learning community or study group.

2. Be certain that your staff development course is inclusive and complete.

3. Focus the study group on a manageable goal.

4. Make staff development courses relevant.

5. Carefully plan and execute in-service and professional development courses.

6. Limit the number of professional development classes.

7. Compensate every group and course participant.

Keywords

Action research

Advisory

Advisory program

In-service education

Institutes in education

Learning community

National Writing Project (NWP)

Problem-based learning (PBL)

Professional development in education

Staff development budgets

Study groups

Study groups in education

Summer institutes in education

Leadership

Leadership is, without question and obviously, complicated and sometimes partly inexplicable, although there are a few guiding principles that may help. These principles come not only from my personal experience but also from my travels around the country to interview successful educational leaders for ASCD's *Educational Leadership* and Phi Delta Kappa's *Kappan.* In the course of doing those interviews, I often visited one or two school districts and, over time, got to know and understand the work of dozens and dozens of interesting, successful, and remarkable school leaders in addition to those I was interviewing for an article.

RULE NUMBER ONE: KNOW WHO YOU ARE AS A SCHOOL LEADER

Articles and books are written every year about the five steps to successful leadership or the eight secrets of leadership or the nine characteristics of leadership revealed by "research" that is in fact almost always anecdotal evidence. As stated in the introduction to this book, most of what we know about good administration is based on best practices, and those practices are genuinely helpful in an area where research is hard to control because of the hundreds of human variables. I've even written some of those "research" pieces myself.

In the end, you need to look carefully at yourself and determine which of the following broad categories best fits your leadership style (not that categorization is ever quite as simple as it sounds): *visionary, renewer,* or *skilled manager.* Of course, there is some overlap between categories, and at different times and under varying circumstances some characteristics may emerge that give the lie to rigid categories. Nevertheless, the odds are pretty good that as a school leader you are dominantly in one of the three categories.

• *Visionaries.* A few leaders are people with great vision who have thought through the kind of department, school, or school district they strongly want to foster, usually not in the mainstream. By force of intellect, determination, charisma, or a combination of two or three of those characteristics, they realize that vision— or crash calamitously. These people are genuine visionaries and are responsible for new ideas in education or in the small number of individualistic and successful schools at both ends of the progressive-conservative spectrum. Howard Gardner's notions of multiple intelligences is an example of an idea; the small schools fostered by Dennis Littky or Deborah Meier and often supported by the Gates Foundation are examples of progressive schools run by visionaries; and the KIPP academies qualify here as highly successful relatively conservative schools.

To succeed as a school visionary, it helps if you plan to remain in the job for at least five years and have reasonable support from above, at least a few "subordinates" who are in sync with you, and the ability to hire several or many people during your first few years on the new job. Of course, visionaries are extremely confident and sometimes defiant of people who try to get in their way.

• *Renewers.* Most leaders have some vision and good managerial skills. They accept jobs in a range of school or district types that roughly fit their personal educational comfort zone and skills. They are open to some change and can grow with new developments, although dramatic or systemic reform is not for them. They are more interested in gradual renewal. These people, solid renewers, are usually in positions of responsibility in the many well-functioning schools and districts across the country that are always open to modest and measured change.

Most of these schools do reasonably well on local and state tests and are heartily approved of by a strong majority of the residents in their communities. There is also much anecdotal evidence by the standards of that community, such as teacher satisfaction or a good record for college acceptance, to support their enviable status.

• *Skilled managers.* Some school leaders have exceptional skills as managers but have difficulty with change, at least if they are expected to be the primary agents of that change. These people accept jobs in places with a long history of success in a particular mode, or they work for visionaries or people with some vision (renewers) doing the very necessary managerial functions.

I have seen many fine managers in schools and districts who do extremely well with assigned tasks as long as they don't have to create the conditions for change. Many assistant principals and school business managers do well in this way. Other managers walk into a very good place and are asked to bring an even higher level of management and organization to a successful school or district.

Managers have often been preceded by reformers or renewers. When change is needed again after several years, the managers move on to another position that requires excellent managing skills, and someone more adept at change or renewal is brought in.

When Sandra Feldman, president of the American Federation of Teachers, announced her retirement in June 2004, some education writers commented that her predecessor, the late Albert Shanker, was an educational visionary, that Feldman was an excellent renewer with a serious interest in educational issues, and that Edward McElroy, the successor to Feldman, was an outstanding manager.

RULE NUMBER TWO: UNDERSTAND THAT ALL LEADERSHIP WORK IS SITUATIONAL

• Before you embark on any new leadership work, try to understand the special circumstances of your individual situation. You might want to ask yourself some questions:

Are your colleagues mostly cooperative or uncooperative?

Are you working with a representative group?

Do you have the material resources you need to proceed?

Are there obstructionist people or other obstacles that will prevent you from doing your work?

Are all or most of the parameters of your prospective task realistic—for instance, time, budget, general goals, and curriculum expectations?

To focus just a bit more sharply on these questions, let's assume for the moment that you are a teacher chairing a committee on a new way to handle discipline in your elementary school. Here are some of the questions you will need to address:

Does the person who asked you to chair the committee have the authority to implement decisions the committee may reach—or at least an excellent chance of getting them approved, if that is required?

Is six weeks enough time to gather the information you need and to have enough thoughtful discussion to make a sound recommendation?

You know that three districts within one hundred miles of you have recently implemented new and successful programs. Will you and your committee have the time and money to visit those places?

Do you have precisely the people you need in your school, district, study group, committee, learning community, or other cohort to get this work done?

Do you need an outside consultant to help you evaluate some new classroom management materials, to show you some better ways to make use of existing data, or to help you gather new information and data that may assist you even more?

Is there a teacher or union leader or administrator who is not in the group but probably should be?

• Take a good look at your skills for your particular leadership task. You need not possess all the skills yourself or even most of the skills needed to get your work done, but do you possess the one or two essential skills absolutely needed for this position? If, for example, the group is relying on you for contact with outside classroom management or math curriculum experts or expects you to be able to explain data or to have a good understanding of the high school schedule, do you possess those skills? For skills that are not essential to the leadership position, do you have people in your group who complement your "weaknesses" or who have the special skills required for some aspects of the work that needs to be done?

RULE NUMBER THREE: BE CERTAIN THAT YOU SHOULD BE IN THE LEADERSHIP POSITION FOR THIS PARTICULAR TASK

You may be the principal or chairperson of your department, and you may even have good skills for this task, but that does not mean you should head every committee or this particular committee. Ask yourself these questions:

Do you have the time for this?

Are you the person with the best skills in the building to head this effort? Perhaps some respected teacher in the math department could head this committee to determine whether the middle school teachers are using the data on student progress well and whether there are other kinds of information and data that would be helpful. You might become a *member* of this committee. You can't head or join every effort to improve things, so make choices. Is this one of the groups you must lead or be part of?

Is it politically wise for you to head or join this committee? Will the teachers or other administrators find it easier to accept the new advisory or science or other program if you are not a member of this committee?

Whatever your position in the school, how much does the success of this committee mean to you? Is this the issue that means the most to you? Will this committee have more credibility if you serve as a helpful member, but one who does not assert himself very often?

Is this perhaps one of three committees this year that you really need to chair? Ask yourself if this is a committee where you feel that your outside contacts, previous experience with the issue under discussion, and strong feelings about establishing this issue as a priority make this a committee you need to lead.

RULE NUMBER FOUR: SET PRIORITIES FOR YOUR WORK AND STICK TO THEM

One of the primary reasons why leaders fail is that they try to please everyone by making too many things priorities, or they make too many priority demands on themselves, with the same failing or subpar result. Whether you are an assistant principal or an assistant superintendent, there are dozens and dozens of things within your sphere of responsibility, but not all of them are priorities.

If, for example, you are the assistant principal in a very large elementary school and have chosen the few items to which you should devote much of your attention and time (certainly with help and guidance from your principal and several other staff members in the building), stick to them for the time they require. Perhaps one or two items were "assigned" to you by the principal, and another one or two are the result of your strongest feelings and convictions.

Be sure your priorities are noticeable to other staff members. Be especially sure that actions you take on them yield some tangible or visible result. Perhaps an occasional report to the faculty or a brief written document will help. It might be that some new materials or equipment are purchased as a result of your committee's work, or some changes are made in the school's schedule. The credit should often go to the committee, not you, although there is no ethical bar to hoping that individual committee members will report in private and completely voluntary conversations that your help and leadership were instrumental in the committee's work. I think it was the Westinghouse company that had the motto, "Progress is our most important product" and not "Our exalted CEO is responsible for everything." Any number of leaders in education, business, and politics have learned that allowing others to receive credit is in the end more powerful than constantly taking credit for oneself.

RULE NUMBER FIVE: LIMIT YOUR PRIORITIES

Having too many priorities means you have no priorities at all—your energy will be too diluted. You should set no more than three or four for the year.

If, for example, you are the chair of the English department, maybe the following are your priorities for this school year: working closely with three teachers up for tenure or continuing appointment later this year; working with a small committee to be chaired by an English teacher colleague to select some new materials for the tenth grade, where the curriculum is not well aligned with the state test; working with the other department chairs to recommend a policy on how the principal assigns budget to the various departments—in fact, you've agreed to chair this committee.

Of course, Mr. English Chairperson, there is that problem with transition from grade 9 to 10; the question of who will teach the senior writing course in the spring is looming; and just last week two of your teachers approached you about attending the state English conference. You'll deal in some reasonable fashion with each of those issues and a few dozen more, but you are clear that the lion's share of your energy and time this year will go to your three top priorities. If one of those other issues or an unexpected one develops or threatens to develop into a crisis, you will shift gears for a short time, but you will make every human effort to stay focused on the three priorities you identified as most important this year.

From time to time, review priorities—certainly at least once each year. Ask yourself if your current priorities continue to be worth pursuing, if some shift in focus is required, or if one or more of your current priorities are coming to an end.

RULE NUMBER SIX: BE THE LAST PERSON TO GET OVERWHELMED

• Remain focused and unflustered, although it is often extremely difficult to do so. This is an important rule of leadership. Whether you are serving as a temporary leader (teacher chairing a committee) or as a permanent leader (principal of a school), the members of the group, school staff, or committee will look to you for focus, equanimity, and a certain amount of guidance and inspiration. If you are overwhelmed, your effectiveness will be limited and your leadership abilities called into question.

• Delegate work, don't take on more work than you can handle with the resources available, and stop occasionally to evaluate where you are in the process. Determine whether you must cut back on some expectations, proceed, or request more resources, but do not allow the task to swallow you up. Any administrator or administrator *pro tem* is expected to work hard, but working to the point that you are not carrying out some serious responsibilities or are inappropriately forgetting them for a time will do no good for you or your school.

In part, this is again a matter of establishing priorities. Many administrators are expected to work forty-five, fifty, or even fifty-five hours each week, but it is neither wise nor necessary to make a habit of working sixty or seventy hours. You cannot be on every committee, go to every evening event, and micromanage all the people and departments in your domain. You need to find some balance and to trust other competent people.

RULE NUMBER SEVEN: WORRY ABOUT ETHICS, LEGALITY, FAIRNESS, AND DECENCY ALL THE TIME

From Enron and Tyco to school scandals ranging from alterations on student tests to the mishandling of funds, the news media are full of stories. Just as business leaders are learning to pay more attention to ethics, so must leaders in schools. Sometimes you may be tempted to make yourself look better by doing something unethical or to use funds in unintended or illegal ways. We're all human, so ethical issues must be in your mind at every important juncture. It helps if this item is on administrative council meetings at regular intervals.

Education is a public trust, and students, staff, and community members look to teachers and administrators to model fair, ethical, decent behavior. Public servants are frequently held to a high standard, often higher than people in the for-profit world. Whether that is fair or not is a separate question, but the fact of it exists. As a school administrator, you are expected to establish a culture of ethical behavior in a school or district—not to mention that it is simply wrong to cheat, embezzle, or commit some other crime or stupidity. You would probably get caught, and it is not worth the loss of your good reputation and career.

RULE NUMBER EIGHT: BE CERTAIN THAT YOUR LEADERSHIP RESPONSIBILITIES AND ASSIGNMENTS ARE APPROPRIATE

• Look carefully at whether the task you have been invited to lead or are considering for yourself can really be accomplished, at least in its present form.

If, for example, there is a problem with your reading scores on a third-grade test and you have been asked to form a committee to determine what can be done—fine. Just get the right people on that committee. If, in contrast, you have been asked to reform the reading program and increase scores by 30 percent in one year, failure is just around the corner. Of course, if you have been asked to chair an excellent committee that will look at the problem and suggest solutions that will very likely increase scores by 12 to 18 percent over three years, you have a good shot—if many of the new or additional resources the committee recommends (better books, some additional training for teachers, and so on) are provided.

• Be careful not to get involved with projects too far above your "pay grade" unless there are very special circumstances. Increasingly and appropriately, teachers and middle-level administrators are being included in decision making and sometimes are invited to chair study groups or committees. Whatever your position, you do not want to chair a committee that has on it several people "above you" and in a position and of a mind to stymie the efforts of the committee.

Suppose that you, a middle school assistant principal, have been asked to chair a districtwide committee on assigning priorities to physical building improvements. The superintendent of buildings and grounds is on the committee, and he reports directly to the superintendent. There are also two principals, four teachers, and two chief custodians on this committee.

The superintendent of schools has met twice with you and the superintendent of buildings and grounds to discuss this committee and has indicated that she will speak briefly to the committee at its first meeting to say that she has great confidence in your ability to do this particular job and that the superintendent of buildings and grounds will serve primarily as a resident expert on technical matters. He has also indicated to the superintendent that he is predisposed to follow most of the committee's suggestions for assigning priorities. This looks good.

In contrast, the same committee without the explicit backing of the superintendent of schools, with an angry superintendent of buildings and grounds who wants to listen to no one but himself, and with one or two principals hanging on tightly to an absolutely fixed agenda is probably heading toward an exercise in futility.

• State what you need for success; if you can't get it, do what you can to remove yourself from the committee, and certainly from the role of chair.

• Don't get ahead of your skills. Most of us need to grow, at our own pace, into the ability to lead a group, chair a department, or become the assistant principal or principal. It takes some time and practice to learn how to make final decisions, to call and prepare for a meeting, to settle a dispute between two angry staff members or factions, or to deliver an unpopular message. Each time you serve in a leadership position, you learn things that make the next time easier. Always think through whether any prospective assignment is within your current skills, experience, and confidence and comfort levels.

Don't be fooled by people who seem to have made a huge leap with some success. Before he became California's governor, Arnold Schwarzenegger served on and chaired many voluntary political committees; supervised large, complex film projects or was close to the people who supervised them; spoke in public dozens of times on topics ranging from fitness to political opinions; became used to wealth and working with large budgets over many years; and spent hundreds if not thousands of hours around politicians in his family and state as well as leading business and entertainment figures in California.

RULE NUMBER NINE: BUILD SUFFICIENT LEADERSHIP CAPACITY

One of the great mistakes we have made too often in education is installing a worthy new program, method, or technique without the requisite leadership capacity—that is, without a substantial and well-trained group of committed people who can work to ensure the continuance of the good program. An advisory system or a new approach to teaching science may fail if the one or perhaps two or three people who were behind it leave the school. Sometimes the only enthusiastic administrator supporting the program leaves the school, and the very few remaining teacher adherents are not enough to continue the deserving program.

Anything new of the least complexity or broad application must have a strong and expansive leadership group behind it. For the purposes of further discussing this rule, let's continue by using the example of a new advisory system; you, a middle school principal, are leading the implementation.

- The advisory system will be one of your three or four priorities for at least two years.

- Be sure to have on board at least six or eight staff members who are enthusiastic initial adherents and are well acquainted with how the system operates and the good it will do for the school. Some, but not all, of these people might be the staff members who first brought the program to your attention.

- Be sure to have as many leaders as possible, formal and informal, behind the new advisory program. It helps if a majority of the administrators and department chairs support the new system. For sure, you want to have several teacher-leaders—people who often chair committees, a union leader, a couple of very highly respected teachers who do not often join committees—supporting the advisory system. The new program will need several years to become part of the school's culture, so you want to broaden the leadership capacity behind it as quickly as possible to give it every chance to flourish.

- Build in as much professional development as possible to support the new program:

  Have a permanent committee on advisory that meets six times each year.

  Offer a brief workshop on advisory each year.

  Circulate articles or buy a couple of copies of any new book on the subject.

  Every second or third year, offer an in-service course on advisory.

  Make advisory part of the mentoring for new teachers.

  Include several new teachers or administrators in advisory training as early as possible.

- Make sure that several committee or study group members speak to any new administrator about the value of the advisory program. It is important to include one or two staff members who are relatively new to the school (second- or third-year people) as members of the advisory committee, even in leadership positions if they are able to do this. The committee should have a revolving membership, so that each year there is room for one or two new members. By the third year of an important new program such as advisory, at least 25 percent of the staff should be very strong adherents, and a very strong staff majority should be counted as supporters of the new program. You are then well on the way to making this program part of the school's culture.

Rules for Leadership

1. Know who you are as a school leader.

2. Understand that all leadership work is situational.

3. Be certain that you should be in the leadership position for this particular task.

4. Set priorities for your work and stick to them.

5. Limit your priorities.

6. Be the last person to get overwhelmed.

7. Worry about ethics, legality, fairness, and decency all the time.

8. Be certain that your leadership responsibilities and assignments are appropriate.

9. Build sufficient leadership capacity.

Keywords

Advisory programs in education
Building leadership capacity
Building leadership capacity in education
Change in schools
Cheating on school tests
Committee leadership skills
Educational administration
Educational leadership
Educational Leadership (ASCD)

Charisma and Creativity in Leadership

I suppose each of us would like to believe there is much of Winston Churchill or FDR or Ronald Reagan in us (pick your model), but it is usually not so, at least not in any great amount. Of course, to get most jobs done, we need to inspire or at least appeal to other people, so we must have some degree of charisma. And to solve a problem of any complexity, even many strictly managerial problems, we must carry some small spark of creativity.

So the question is, How do most of us get the job done? Every educational leader quickly realizes that he or she has to enlist the aid of other staff members to get things done. You must find elements of charisma and creativity in other people either to complement your skills or to supplant them if you are not taking the lead in this particular effort. Of course, there is also much to be said for pooling several people's diverse talents and employing mechanisms for extracting a final conclusion from this interesting mix in which the most creative ideas have been welcomed—though they do not often survive in unalloyed form.

Before you go on the hunt for people to fill in for your "deficiencies," do not underestimate yourself. Somehow you were chosen for your job, and it is unlikely that you were recommended for your dull, uninspiring, totally predictable ways! Still, you are not always the right person with precisely the right creativity and charisma for every task, and, as I've said several times in this book, your time and energy are limited. In fact, even the most charismatic and creative administrators learn that often it is wise to share the credit and responsibility for accomplishments. You don't build leadership capacity by making yourself the fulcrum of every program.

RULE NUMBER ONE: FIND THE RIGHT PERSON OR PEOPLE FOR THE TASK

Perhaps you have a faculty meeting coming up, and three topics will be on the agenda. Don't hog the limelight. You will appear in front of your faculty often enough during your tenure as administrator. Instead, find the staff member who has the needed charisma and creativity (and respect for others' creativity) to lead the discussion of each topic.

For instance, if one of the topics is to reach a final decision on the two staff development courses that will be offered this summer for your school's staff, allow the energetic, well-liked, and respected teacher-chairperson of the committee that considered this issue to introduce it. Have one or two enthusiastic members of that committee remind the staff of the virtues of the three courses the committee has recommended, and let the teacher-chairperson, chosen because she has some charisma, leadership ability, and clout with the faculty, handle the vote to reduce three courses to two.

Using this approach, you will have decentralized leadership and taken advantage of the skills of two or three teachers at this faculty meeting. Whatever creativity and charisma the members of this committee had, along with their skills for distilling a great deal of information down to three solid choices, was just on display at the faculty meeting. And you were the proud administrator behind this—not the administrator with little charisma, just one who was wise enough to use skilled staff in the right place.

Over several years in your position, you will have used many staff members, for different purposes that fit their skills, in positions of trust and authority. You will enjoy a growing reputation as someone strong and confident enough to share power with numerous staff members, and you will have come to know staff better through setting up these committees and distributing administrative responsibilities. The days of the all-powerful leader are gone—in education, business, politics, everywhere. The school administrator remains extremely important as the person in the midst of many activities, but it is often the effort of the team or staff that gets things done in a complex and ever-changing education world.

RULE NUMBER TWO: BALANCE COMMITTEE MEMBERSHIP

I'll continue with the staff development example from Rule Number One, but we'll go back in time.

> There will be three districtwide professional development courses this summer, each lasting three weeks, and they have been established by a districtwide committee. Your school has been granted funds to offer two additional courses just for your teachers, one for a week and the other for two weeks. In the next four weeks, you need to establish the committee for gathering information from your faculty and reducing that information to three final choices that will be presented to the whole faculty for a vote on the final two courses.

• The first consideration is whether you, the principal, should be on the committee. If you decide that your presence on the committee is not wise and that you are willing to live with the decisions of the committee, you should at least be at the initial meeting to establish any necessary guidelines, including any preferences for courses you may have, and to tell the committee members how you can help them or enhance their work, should they need to call on you. Even if you're not a member, you need to show your enthusiasm for the committee.

• The second consideration is how far you should go in choosing members of the committee. If you hope the committee will approach the issue in some unexpected ways, choose a teacher-chairperson who has some charisma and either is reasonably creative or who likes and will promote creative thinking. You may wish to appoint one department chairperson to the committee, perhaps a chair who also likes creativity, and then leave the selection of the rest of the members to those two people, giving them the guidelines that no more than seven people can serve and that at least three different grades or disciplines must be represented.

Of course, you could work with the two people you appointed to choose the other committee members, or you could appoint a third member—or even the entire committee. The point here is for you to think through how much control you want or need over this committee. Sometimes it makes sense to give up all or most control; other times you will want enough control to establish some fairly narrow guidelines. This is your judgment call. The only inalterable advice is never to set up a committee over which you exercise 100 percent control. If you need that level of control over a decision, rely on your own charisma and creativity to "sell" whatever is at stake directly to the staff.

Please note: When I use the word *charisma,* I don't mean that each school should have three Bette Midlers on staff who can jump on tables and wow the faculty. I do mean that each staff has several people who both command respect and have "endearing" (somewhat charismatic) personalities, and their skills should be used. When I say "creativity," I don't mean that each school needs to have someone whose "work" or personality could be displayed at the Museum of Modern Art. However, each school has people who like to suggest ideas that are out of the mainstream, and these ideas can sometimes be adopted or, more typically, revised somewhat to fit the school's needs. Of course, you need to exercise some caution and not choose the school's well-known one "stubborn-crazy" for committee work.

• Any guidelines you give the committee should be as broad as possible, so as not to stifle its work. The course preferences, if any, that you state to the committee will carry some weight, but the committee need not include them in the final three if they determine that some other courses are more urgently needed. If you really want one of your preferences to be included in some form, be honest and say that to the committee at the outset.

RULE NUMBER THREE: USE BRAINSTORMING

Brainstorming—asking a group to make many initial suggestions and neither rejecting nor judging any of them—is a proven but underused, highly creative activity and one that will often lead to several good starting places. You can hold a brainstorming session at a department meeting or K–4 meeting with ten or twelve teachers, a principal's meeting with just a few other administrators, or even a meeting of an entire faculty. At least four things happen during brainstorming:

- Lots of ideas are put on the table.
- Participants' creativity is sparked by hearing other people's suggestions, thus leading them to come up with yet more ideas.
- People are emboldened to speak even if their idea is "wildly" creative, because these are just ideas, not fully developed plans.
- Some people who do not frequently speak out will take the risk, usually after several other people have spoken.

The following are some general guidelines for ensuring effective brainstorming sessions.

- Have someone take notes during brainstorming. That way, all the possibilities, including yours, are up for later consideration at the first meeting of the group, study group, or committee that will review the brainstorming suggestions. If possible, have the person taking notes at the brainstorming session read them back before the meeting ends to make sure you have an accurate version of the proposals. If that's not possible, circulate the notes the next day and ask if any notes are inaccurate. Within a day or two the people who proposed ideas should contact the person who took the notes to clear up any possible misunderstanding at the group or committee meeting that will take place very soon after the brainstorming session.

- Form the study group or committee within days of the brainstorming session. More often than not, you should not chair this committee, but should choose the chair—some reliable and fair-minded teacher or "subordinate" administrator. The chairperson should choose the other committee members in a very transparent way, perhaps asking for volunteers or approaching two people and asking them to find another two people. To the extent possible, all the guidelines suggested earlier in this chapter and book about personal skills and not having only the usual suspects on the committee obtain here.

- Give general feedback to the staff at intervals, assuring them of progress and the careful consideration of all ideas. Staff members want to feel that their ideas were considered. The committee should, of course, consider each idea as they go through the process of accepting, combining, and rejecting suggestions.

RULE NUMBER FOUR: USE CHARISMA AND CREATIVITY CAREFULLY

I've written elsewhere in this book about building leadership capacity in programs that are worthwhile. One of the pitfalls, particularly of charisma, is that people and programs can at first have enormous appeal that does not stand up to the test of time in daily application in a classroom or in administrative work. It's always necessary to look carefully at novel ideas to see what revisions, if any, they need.

As administrator, you are the final check on ensuring that the committee has crafted the proposed presentation to the faculty in a way that is balanced—both novel and realistic. You are predisposed to support this committee and have been kept informed of their work if you were not a committee member. However, just before presentation, it is wise to act as a devil's advocate and ask some questions:

Does the program meet the needs initially established by the committee?

Is this even better than anything the committee imagined at the outset? What makes it better?

Does the new idea have the rigor you want?

What revisions, if any, might have to be made to make this idea work?

Is this a serious program, one that represents the best we can produce, or are we being seduced by some very creative ideas that won't work in the classroom or in administrative practice?

Do we have the resources to implement these proposals, or at least many of them?

Have we come as close to the ideal program as possible at this time?

Is there anything else we should consider before we proceed to final presentation?

Please note: Balance the information in Rule Number Four with the suggestions in Rule Number Five.

RULE NUMBER FIVE: AIM HIGH

Charisma and creativity will often cause you to aim very high, and that is good.

• Never start the consideration of an issue or program with the limitations. Give full opportunity at the outset to ideal solutions to problems. Telling the group that there is very little money or that it must restrict the effort because of time, resources, community tolerance, faculty limits, or other obstacles will place boundaries on thinking. In the end, you must come back to the real world, but not at the beginning.

If, for example, you want to look at a new physical education program for the middle school or how cooperative learning can work in grades 4 and 5, start by considering the best and most complete programs you can find. Your attitude should be, "Let's come as close to that wealthy private school's program as we can," and not, "Let's start with reality and not delude ourselves into thinking we can escape our all-too-real limits."

• Once you've considered the programs with greatest appeal and formulated a proposal close to the ideal for your circumstances, think about every possible means of funding it: shifting resources, applying for a grant, asking the central administration or board for additional funds, appealing to the parents' organization or local businesses for whatever you need, and so on. Again, you may not get everything you want, and you may have to make some modifications, but you'll have done all you can to produce the best new program under your local circumstances—stretched to their absolute limits.

It is always important, even in daily planning, for administrators to aim high and to encourage other staff members to work toward ideals or high standards. When we look at the most successful programs in any region of the country, inevitably we find that several smart people with charisma, creativity, and determination were at their center. They thought big and ended up creating something better or more interesting than they or others had anticipated at the outset. But because schools are very human, messy, demanding places, we also find people who were able to tweak or revise or rework those big ideas into a form that really worked.

Rules for Creativity and Charisma in Leadership

1. Find the right person or people for the task.

2. Balance committee membership.

3. Use brainstorming.

4. Use charisma and creativity carefully.

5. Aim high.

Keywords

Brainstorming
Building leadership capacity
Charisma in education
Creativity in education
Committee membership
Committee work
Committee work in education

Conducting good meetings
Decentralized leadership in education
Excellence in faculty meetings
Faculty meetings
Faculty meetings K–12
Sharing leadership in education

Supervision of Staff

The first question you need to ask yourself is, "Why am I supervising this particular person?" Are you fulfilling a contractual obligation? Is the person up for tenure or continuing appointment this year? Are you just doing a *pro forma* job with someone who is very solid and experienced and requires relatively little formal supervision? Are you trying to work with this person in a collegial way to help her grow or improve in her work? Are you trying to bring about some change or renewal in your school or district through supervision?

Obviously, the most desirable goal for supervision is to help staff members grow and improve as professionals. This is especially important in a time when school work is changing. Many states now have alternative certification. Schools are changing as more magnet schools, charter schools, and small schools for special purposes come into being each year. Other influences, such as technology, new forms of assessment, differentiated instruction, state standards, differential salaries and bonuses, and schools built around a mentoring concept, alter our notion of what, exactly, a school should be like.

When I visit or read about districts I've not been in for just a few years, I often learn that the mission of the place has changed. There is a smaller special interest school within the larger school, or several special interest schools have developed in the district. From pre–Advanced Placement (AP) classes or early International Baccalaureate (IB) programs to specialized science or performing arts programs, from remedial test drill classes to work-study offerings and schools that feature co-operative learning or problem-based learning, change is everywhere. Even in schools where test preparation is dominant, administrators and other staff members are promoting technology, small-group student learning, teacher study groups to deconstruct standards and tests, tightly focused instruction, and many other techniques to enhance scores.

Too many supervisors are doing their supervisory work for the schools that existed twenty or more years ago. Too much supervision continues to take the form of an ostensible expert observing a very narrow, and not always relevant, slice of a staff member's work, usually two or three classes a year, and then making a decision about the continuation of that staff member in his or her job or reaching a set of conclusions about a staff member's degree of accomplishment.

In this chapter, I suggest several ways in which supervision can be expanded, particularly under Rule Number Three. I do understand that some school districts have their own historical methods or contractual agreements about how supervision should be conducted and that some supervisors are not yet ready to try something quite different. However, I strongly encourage administrators and teachers to begin learning about the many alternatives available in supervision, and hope this chapter will stimulate that learning.

RULE NUMBER ONE: MAKE SURE YOU ARE IN THE RIGHT SCHOOL OR DISTRICT

If you are a terrific manager of mainstream schools where modest renewal is welcomed, but have ended up in a rather progressive school where considerable change and frequent collegial supervision are embraced, you are in the wrong place to be a supervisor. This would be a dramatic misplacement of your talents. It is unlikely to happen if you and the interviewers were careful, but I cite this as a way of saying that supervision is as situational as everything else in education. It is very hard for a traditional supervisor (a manager with a mild penchant for cautious renewal) to work with zealous change agents, and vice versa.

- Learn as quickly as you can what forms of supervision are expected, by contract or history. The next step is to learn how much variation will be tolerated, particularly in circumstances where tenure or continuation are not involved.
- Show staff that you are interested in change and want much of that interest to find expression in supervision techniques, but don't go faster than your experience and the staff's tolerance will allow. Shooting stars burn out rather quickly. If

you are in the early stages of your work as a supervisor, you are probably trying to create a harmonious situation, one that blends your needs and skills, the school's culture, and your ability to shape that culture—probably not reform it wholesale, but shape it somewhat.

RULE NUMBER TWO: MEET WITH YOUR SUPERVISOR AND YOUR STAFF

For the purposes of discussing this rule, let's suppose you are a new elementary principal who has been carefully and thoughtfully assured by your immediate supervisor that new forms of supervision are possible.

- Begin thinking through meeting with your staff in a collegial way to determine what forms of supervision might help. Be cautious about your relationship with your boss, Ms. New Elementary Principal. Lots of people want to seem more progressive than they really are. That's why I emphasize a careful and thoughtful discussion as well as a follow-up conversation just before you introduce or elicit ideas for reform in supervision. Of course, if your supervisor publicly announces that she is supportive of responsible change, all the better.

- Meet with individuals or with small groups to see what ideas they have for supervision, always assuring them that the goal is professional growth and improvement. Would four or five teachers like to work together, observing each other, perhaps taping some lessons or parts of lessons? Would others prefer to work on some individual area of growth best done alone or with just one like-minded colleague? Some teachers, of course, really like traditional supervision or are simply not ready for a change. Tell them when you're coming to their classroom, have a preconference, watch a carefully designed lesson, and schedule a postconference. But hold out the possibility for trying something new in time, perhaps with a colleague or two.

- Consider drawing up a simple agreement, one-half page, that states what will happen in your supervisory relationship. This agreement is always informal and contains the final statement, "This agreement is always open to change as conditions change." If the supervision is aimed at growth, with little or preferably no issue of tenure or continuation, keep it as unthreatening as possible. This agreement will in no way be used as part of a final evaluation, unless both parties agree that it is useful to do so. Otherwise, it is only a way to memorialize the broad outlines of what you and the teachers with whom you have this special arrangement this year will try to accomplish.

RULE NUMBER THREE: SEEK COLLEGIAL METHODS OF SUPERVISION

• Try coaching. A coaching relationship will often work if you have considerable expertise and are working with a staff member with less expertise, or if you have particularly good coaching skills and can see where a teacher might need some help, encouragement, or specific training. If you are, say, a very experienced elementary principal with a strong background in math or classroom management, you might, after observations or in formal or informal conversations, start the dialogue by asking a less experienced teacher what he did very well and what he felt did not go so well in a math lesson or in some aspect of classroom management.

If you and your staff member agree on a coaching relationship, you do not usually issue mandates when trying to influence the teacher, but are more prone to guide, to ask questions, to make suggestions. Sentences often start with "What do you think about trying . . . ?" or "What might happen if . . . ?" Usually it is wise to focus on just one or two features of what you've observed. Coaching is a conversation between two people who have the same goal: to help the staff member grow and improve.

• Use coaching in peer supervision. You could set this up, but typically you do not engage in direct observations, only in group meetings where there is discussion of how things are going and what might improve the technique. A group of, say, four math or English teachers in a middle school or all five of the third-grade teachers in an elementary school become a peer coaching group. They agree on a schedule to observe each other and set up some ground rules for the observations.

Generally, there are three simple guidelines for peer coaching. First, the teachers agree on one or two aspects of their classroom work for primary or exclusive focus. Perhaps the math teachers want to determine if they are getting enough accurate feedback from students and if there is any pattern as to which students dominate the class. Of course, they'll discuss methods for correcting problems and may even use you as a resource for that.

Second, all or most of the teacher feedback should start with questions, although the use of more direct approaches increases as the group develops considerable trust and mutual respect. No effort is made to humiliate or overwhelm a colleague with more information than is helpful in a particular session.

Third, everything is confidential within the coaching group. Out-of-group talk, except very general conversation intended to encourage others to try the technique, is the kiss of death.

• Make frequent, often brief classroom visits. This technique is best used with a teacher with whom you have a strong relationship, as it requires considerable trust right from the beginning. The idea here is to "drop in" often enough to gain a real idea of how the teacher works and to have many conversations about his work. It may take several years for most of your staff to agree to an arrangement like this.

Some supervisors and teachers find that dropping in eight to twelve times a year for ten or twenty minutes yields a much more accurate picture than three full-period staged visits. The teacher must be confident enough to tolerate the fact that you will sometimes see her at her best, but will also see her when she has a headache and doesn't feel like teaching. Frequent short notes and conversations, many of them reassuring, help in this relationship. Of course, the teacher may ask that once a year you attend a full class, particularly if something special is going on.

• Use portfolios. Portfolios have become more common in the last fifteen years and can be useful with both beginning and more experienced staff. Any staff member can work with a portfolio—including a principal, teacher, or school aide—but the portfolios will vary with position and the particular agreement.

An assistant principal might agree to maintain a portfolio just on two important goals she has established with her principal for that year. If one goal is to establish more and better community relations, she would certainly have a list of all the meetings she attended with parent groups, businesspeople, local politicians, and other community figures as well as the outcomes of those meetings. For instance, if as a result of the assistant principal's entreaties some local business group agreed to donate several computers to the school or release a few employees for several hours each month to tutor students, that information would be in the portfolio, along with materials verifying that these things actually happened.

An important issue here is to reach reasonable agreement on what will be in the portfolio and what its limits will be. The portfolio could contain, for example, lists, letters, a video or DVD, a record of meetings attended, reference to a Web site, photographs of student projects, or examples of student written work. Any agreement with a staff member should be focused, so that compiling the portfolio does not become an onerous task. For instance, a teacher might collect materials only on math or writing or a particular four-week unit. The portfolio collection should be very manageable, often a pleasure to maintain, and supportive of the one or two agreed-on areas of growth or concern.

Portfolios are an excellent way to work with staff in a special or unusual setting. In a work-study program or a magnet school that promotes student performance and exhibitions, there are features of the work that are different from that produced in a more traditional setting. Using video, photographs, a blog, a Web site, testimony from outside observers, and other methods may give a far more accurate picture of the teacher's or assistant principal's work than more traditional supervision.

• Work with a small group or team on a very specific issue or perceived problem. This approach to supervision builds in all of the pleasures that come from social contact—not to be underestimated in even the most serious enterprises—and allows a teaching supervisor to become part of the group working toward a common goal. This technique is often used when staff members are going to observe each other.

For instance, a group of teachers may be concerned about the probability that a particular teacher, or the teacher and a few students, is dominating the classroom conversation and that there is not enough inclusive discussion and interaction. The concern has gone beyond one department, and a group of ten teachers representing three departments would like to work on this.

The group meets to talk about this issue and arranges a schedule of visits, usually with two group members as observers. The supervisors, in this case the math, art, and music department chairs, who each teach two or three classes, are part of the group of ten. They discuss how they will keep track of who is talking in class and for what purpose. They could tape the class or use a formal "scoring" technique such as Amidon-Flanders, or they might discuss ways of doing this impressionistically. Often it helps if two teachers observe the same class. Sometimes this in-school group work will lead to the formation of a study group; one of the early tasks would be to do some modest research to learn what observation techniques are out there and which one will work best for this group.

The goals for the group might be to determine how well the teacher was able to control and "distribute" the conversation, whether the particular distribution was effective, and whether or not the teacher had an accurate sense of that effectiveness. In addition, the teacher needs to know how dominant he or she was and when that dominance seemed to help or hurt the lesson. In effect, each member of the team serves as a coach-observer.

Please note: Just as an aside, I have both participated in such teams and been observed, and have frequently been surprised to learn that I and many others when teaching do not agree with the observers—who usually are more accurate than the teacher. In my case, after some skillful feedback from colleagues, I began to "hear" what they said they observed. If the lesson was taped, I viewed it and almost always came to agree with what the more objective observers saw.

• Expand the team or group's work into a study group. In this case, teachers receive in-service credit or some other compensation because the group work makes more demands on the participants' time. To discuss this approach, I'll use a new example:

> In this district, several teachers and administrators are interested in differentiated instruction because many students from another country have moved into the district in the past three years, and they require different levels of instruction and even different approaches. Several new students have entered the district with advanced skills, especially in math, whereas others are having problems because they do not yet speak or read well in English. They are also accustomed to teaching methods very different from those practiced in your school.

The study group has designed a course of inquiry and study for fifteen weeks, thirty hours after school except for two school visits to other campuses by three members of the study group. Work also includes the following:

Reading three or four relevant articles

Bringing in two local experts, perhaps parents who do not charge anything, to speak to the group

Reading one or two chapters of special interest in books on differentiated instruction

Crafting several lessons that will be tried in the classroom.

Of course, peer observation will be one important method by which the group will evaluate its efforts with these new students.

At the end of the course, the group will make a presentation to the faculty about what it has learned and will determine if additional in-service work should be recommended. All the books, articles, and lesson materials and the two videotapes of lessons that were judged instructive for demonstrating what was effective or problematic will be available to the entire faculty through the school library.

If the students in the school are at many learning levels and represent a wide variety of instructional challenges (a phenomenon more and more common in American schools), the first study group of eight or ten teachers and administrators will lead to more groups and increased in-service instruction. This, of course, takes us back to the chapter on staff development (Chapter Five).

• Form a small problem-based learning (PBL) group. This variation on the study group, which usually comprises four to six teachers, forms around a question of compelling interest and connects with supervision. This is typically a group of experienced teachers for whom neither tenure nor continuing service is an issue. The supervisor can either be a member of this group or can meet with the group from time to time. In either case, the PBL effort replaces traditional supervision for a period of time, sometimes for as long as half a year.

One example of PBL would be a group of five fourth-grade teachers and the elementary reading teacher trying to figure out how best to help the one or two students in each of the fourth-grade classes who continue to struggle with reading. In PBL there is never a single or obvious answer, at least at first. The teachers are honestly puzzled over how to proceed, because the reading and classroom teachers have tried several techniques to little avail.

> *Step 1: Frame the question.* "Given that several competent professionals have worked with these students who remain well below grade level, what possibilities remain or can we discover that might help?"

> *Step 2: Brainstorm and review.* The group looks at what has been tried, what variations might work, and what else could be done. Teachers should be as creative as possible here. Ideas that seem slightly farfetched at first may contain a kernel of help when considered later.

> *Step 3: Collect all the relevant information.* In this case, the group might look at test data, articles on working with struggling readers, and insights gained from discussions with previous teachers, parents, the students themselves, and outside experts, if available and needed.

> *Step 4: Devise a plan or plans for action.* The group bases the plan(s) on what it has learned. In this example, it is unlikely that one plan will fit all.

Step 5: Carry out the plan(s) on a trial basis. The idea is to try the plans for enough time to yield either positive results or continued frustration—say, six to twelve weeks. In this example, the reading or classroom teacher will determine progress by conducting careful evaluation at intervals of about three weeks.

Step 6: Meet again formally to review progress and make suggestions. If the plans are working, fine. In many cases, some tweaking will be required, or a slightly smaller PBL group may do a second round to consider what to do about the two very recalcitrant cases.

Provided that the meetings and other work are not very burdensome, PBL work is just part of the normal work day, using meeting and planning times that are part of the school schedule. When the work becomes more burdensome, many school districts provide for one in-service credit, a small stipend, or some other modest compensation for meetings and work that had to occur outside of school hours.

Teachers and administrators in many places have used PBL to good effect. In fact, it has yielded innovations that have helped struggling students. Many teachers have even taught their students how to use PBL in a classroom unit.

Rules for Supervision of Staff

1. Make sure you are in the right school or district.

2. Meet with your supervisor and your staff.

3. Seek collegial methods of supervision.

Keywords

Action research
Amidon-Flanders
Coaching teachers
Cognitive coaching
Mentoring
Peer assessment in schools
Peer coaching in schools
Peer supervision in schools
Portfolios for administrators

Portfolios for school supervision
Portfolios for teachers
Problem-based learning
Study groups
Study groups for teacher supervision
Supervision of school staff
Supervision of teachers
Supervision techniques in schools

Statistical Data and Other Forms of Information

D o you have to be a math major or a statistician to survive in administration in the twenty-first century? Of course not, but you do have to have a healthy regard for data intended to help school staff, a healthy skepticism of data, and a basic understanding of what you are looking at when you receive the results of various tests or other statistical information. You also need to have considerable respect for nonstatistical forms of information, as well as good antennae for misinformation, partial information, and skewed information.

The basic points here are that you must take data very seriously; be able to analyze the data, often with help from a local expert or two; and seek out and make careful judgments about many other forms of information, ranging from informed teacher opinions to local gossip. You cannot get the whole picture of a student, a group of students, a school, or a school district from statistical data alone, although all forms of numerical data are of value and constitute an important part of the entire picture.

You need to know, for example, that one fourth-grade class had three different teachers this year, that six children from Laos who spoke no English arrived in October, that the first-grade teacher who has consistently produced excellent results in reading was out for surgery the eight weeks before the test was administered, and that the grapevine says that this year's math test was much easier than those of the last two years.

Before I present any rules, I want to put the data issue in context. The data that come from the state or federal government, particularly on mandated tests, need to be understood, although that may require some help from local experts or state officials. Commonly, schools are purchasing software as a way to deal with an amazing variety of data: budgets, attendance, report cards, scores from teacher-constructed tests, and even information about students' home contact information, health background, names of previous teachers, and discipline history.

Because the focus in this book is on building-level administrators and central office curriculum and instruction staff, I recommend that administrators and teachers aggressively seek to get on the committees that select the software programs for local use or to communicate in other ways what data will be helpful. Once software is purchased, you are stuck with it for some period of time.

If you and your teachers want to know some or all of a student's previous teachers, test scores, and even indicators of areas of deficiency and skill or other helpful information, you need to communicate that to the information technology person and any other person who recommends data software purchases. As mentioned, it is even better if you, or logical staff representatives reporting to you, are on the selection committee to make your case and to develop a good understanding of the trends in new purchases. You do not need to be a software or data expert to serve on a purchasing committee, but you do need to have a clear idea of what information will be helpful in your school or district.

There is only one overarching principle here: all data must be easily available and understandable, or people will not use them. If the program is very complex or if the only computer available to access data is in the guidance office, staff will make little or no use of it. Within the bounds of privacy and security, you must make the data conveniently available to teachers and administrators. To the extent that data from the state or federal government are "unhelpful," you should lodge a formal complaint and ask for changes or help in understanding any confusing or less-than-clear information.

RULE NUMBER ONE: DETERMINE WHAT DATA YOU ARE RECEIVING NOW AND THEIR VALUE

Regardless of your circumstances, your first step is to determine what data you are already receiving. Are they of value to you in addressing your school's particular concerns? Are there data or information you are not receiving that would help you?

If, for example, student attendance has been a problem and you are receiving very general or sketchy data, you will want to do something about that. Knowing the number of students absent each day may be a good starting point, but it is not enough. A school or district might have a goal of 95 percent attendance each day, and you are now running about 88 percent on average.

What questions should you ask of the responsible attendance officials, ranging from a part-time attendance secretary to an attendance official with a staff, that will yield helpful information? Here are some possibilities:

What is the absence percentage for each grade?

Are there any unusual circumstances, such as a small group of students who have serious illnesses?

Are there days of the week when attendance is especially low? Why? What must be done to find out the reasons if the answer is not known?

Are there particular students who do not seem to be ill, yet have poor attendance?

These and a dozen other questions might improve your data and your effectiveness in either explaining the problem or dealing with it.

RULE NUMBER TWO: DETERMINE WHAT DATA WILL SERVE YOUR PURPOSE AND WHO SHOULD COLLECT THEM

What data do you want to cross your desk at regular intervals? Your answer will, of course, depend on what you see as your priorities and what priorities have been set by the district. For the areas of greatest concern to you—for example, attendance and discipline—perhaps you will want weekly or biweekly or even daily reports; receiving reports every three to five weeks on progress in newly instituted testing programs would be appropriate. Although you will want all sorts of data to cross your desk, you will never lose sight of your four priority areas.

You also want to learn about important data that go to other staff members in whom you have confidence, but surely in less detail and at even greater intervals than data that come directly to you. Trying to stay abreast in a deep and detailed way with the twenty or thirty reports that go to various people in your school or district would sap your mental energy and prevent you from performing other parts of your job well. One way to control the "inflow" of data from others would be to request that you be notified immediately when there is unusual movement in the data or when any staff member has something important to report on that relates to any of your four areas of special interest.

Have you established *who*, exactly, will gather the data and information you want on each of your areas of concern? Have you met with those people frequently enough, so that they know what sort of data and information you want at regular intervals and feel comfortable contacting you immediately about a serious problem or important success? For areas of less concern, but not necessarily of less importance, do the people gathering the data and information know when they should alert you to a problem or success of unusual significance?

Suppose, for example, that you and your high school staff have agreed to use, whenever possible, several measures other than school detention as part of your student management approach. Perhaps you have been averaging fifteen detention assignments per week, a 50 percent reduction in the use of detention, since the inception of a new program. You have established as a guideline with an assistant principal that you want to know immediately or within two school days whenever detention assignments average twenty-two or more in any five-day period. That is, you have established a specific indicator of when you and the assistant principal will meet to determine if this is a trend, if one or two teachers are assigning a lot of detentions, and if this number is warranted for a limited period of time.

RULE NUMBER THREE: DETERMINE WHAT DATA AND INFORMATION YOU WILL REQUIRE FOR THE SCHOOL AND WHO SHOULD RECEIVE THEM

• Meet with the staff members who should collect data and information. Emphasize that you are interested in both. Start by asking such questions as the following:

What do you collect now?

What is lacking, and what help do you require?

How will you collect and analyze the data and information you gather?

Over what period of time will you gather the data and information?

How can we make intelligent use of nonstatistical information?

How can we review collection of numerical data and other forms of information to make sure the effort is not reaching diminishing returns or becoming too burdensome?

Do you maintain careful records for a particular area for one semester, a school year, three years, or longer?

How can you best present that data and information to me and others?

How often should we meet to review what you've collected?

• Be sure to emphasize that you are very interested in what staff members are saying, reports they've written, and any rumors going around. The data are very important, but again, they are not the entire story in a school. If a group of unhappy parents is meeting to question the new science program and rumors of unrest are beginning to float around, staff members should alert you as soon as possible.

• Think through the kinds of questions you might ask of people reporting to you that will reveal the limits of the data or go beyond the data. Here are some examples:

How much information do the reading results give us on how to help a particular student?

Can we get breakout data on Johnny or Mary that will tell us something about fluency or vocabulary or comprehension?

What do we know about Johnny's attendance?

Who should follow up on the four students who are absent at least two Mondays each month? What's going on there?

Can you tell me a bit about Mary and her family? Is it true that her father is in the hospital for a long stay and that the mother takes her out of school each Friday to visit him during his physical therapy? How can we help with that? Is she enrolled in our Monday after-school makeup class?

What can you tell me about the rumor that George (a very fine and experienced science teacher who produces great statistical and anecdotal results each year) is considering leaving to become a teacher in a nearby district? Is there anything we can do to influence him to remain here?

RULE NUMBER FOUR: DETERMINE THE BEST WAYS TO PRESENT DATA

Your goal is to enable the maximum number of people to understand relevant data quickly, easily, and effectively.

• Ask yourself and your staff questions about presentation. The following are some examples:

Are we getting a lot of data in a format that is helpful? If not, can we take the present format and make it better?

Should we use a bar graph, a pie chart, a line graph, or some other useful method to express the data?

What sorts of lists and columns will help?

How can we break the data down so that they are useful to the classroom teacher?

Should the technical presentation be preceded by a short narrative summary?

Should the data be followed by some narrative interpretation or questions?

Would a spoken presentation with charts or slides help?

• Get help if you need it. Remember, if you are not an expert at working with statistical data, there are people in or near every school district who are: computer experts; math teachers; staff members who have taken two or three courses in statistics; experts at a local community college or university; community experts, especially parents who will volunteer their time; and others. Yes, you need to understand the data once they are explained to you or put in a helpful format, but no, you need not have a Ph.D. in statistics!

• Hold a workshop or two. Such a workshop, which could use faculty meeting time, would focus on how to look at and interpret some of the important data you and your staff receive. Often these workshops will be conducted by a member of your school district's staff with general expertise in statistics and data. Another possibility would be for the reading teacher, a guidance counselor, a math teacher, or some central office administrator to conduct all or part of a workshop in her or his area of expertise. If the data do not pertain to the whole staff, invite only those staff members who have an interest, although other staff members could attend voluntarily.

RULE NUMBER FIVE: UNDERSTAND YOUR STATE'S STANDARDS, TESTS, AND TEST RESULT INFORMATION

Many states have excellent standards, some states have tests that are better than others, and the data provided as a result of the tests vary widely from state to state in terms of their usefulness and timeliness. Teachers often complain that the data they receive are too general to help with instruction or are received too late in the school year to be useful.

Whether or not you like your state's standards and tests and any curriculum help provided, you need to live with them until they are changed. Perhaps you will want to be part of the group that brings about responsible change, but to do that you will need to gain a firm understanding of the standards, tests, and curriculum materials. In fact, every school district needs to gain that understanding by deconstructing the standards, previous tests based on those standards, and any material provided by the state to help with current tests.

One intelligent and helpful way to conduct this deconstruction is to have a small group of teachers in a subject area or grade level analyze the standards and tests. This focuses the teachers on these materials and helps them determine how best to construct local curriculum that will yield good scores and leave time for other activities they consider worthwhile.

Such group analysis, of course, is an excellent way to go about any curriculum work, state test or no state test, but under the NCLB law, each school must make a serious effort to perform well on mandated tests, and cooperative staff efforts have yielded good results in many places. Your district may also be able to get help from state officials or regional or county representatives. However you work, the emphasis is always on getting good results from your students.

RULE NUMBER SIX: EMPHASIZE RESULTS IN YOUR DATA GATHERING AND ANALYSIS

As we discussed under Rule Number Two, as an administrator, you'll have your four chief areas that you'll follow. You will receive data and information at regular intervals and at any time additional data or new information is needed. The whole point of your receiving data and information is to help you focus on how to achieve better results.

Let's suppose you are an assistant principal in a high school, and one of your priorities is to follow information on class cutting. You probably generate a daily report, but you certainly will want to look at weekly and monthly reports, make comparisons among blocks, periods, or classes and days, and follow up on students, teachers, or particular classes that have a greater problem than others. The numbers will tell you a great deal, but you also need to get anecdotal information from teachers, students, parents, guidance counselors, your social worker, and others to understand the complete picture.

If one teacher is extremely lax about taking attendance or has a far greater percentage of students cutting than the school average, you need to learn just what is going on and determine some reasonable and effective steps to ameliorate the problem. Perhaps one teacher has a disproportionate number of problem students in his or her class, particularly students who have a long history of class cutting. It may be that one teacher gives a very difficult quiz each Thursday, and several students who are unprepared simply don't go to class.

You note that a junior who does not usually cut classes has missed period 6 music for three days. When you speak to the teacher, you learn that the boy's former girlfriend is in the class, as is her new boyfriend. Is there another section of music this boy can attend? Will this work in his schedule? Would it help to talk to all three of the students involved? What does the "aggrieved" boy think will work? Are there other possible solutions?

For areas of great importance, collect data and information over time. Have there been changes in, for example, attendance, reading scores, Back-to-School Night attendance, or participation in science competitions over the past three or four years? Given all the information you have gathered, what actions have you taken? Are further actions required and warranted?

When something is obviously wrong—say, reading scores have gone down for the third consecutive year in grade 5, some action is *required*, although it need not necessarily be action beyond what a classroom teacher can do with some help or guidance. Again, go beyond the numbers and raise questions.

Have several new students who are considerably below the usual class average registered in grade 5 each of the last three years? If so, what will help? You might ask some of these questions:

Should there be more reading instruction from the regular classroom teacher, assignment of an aide with skills in reading instruction six hours each week, help from the reading specialist, or additional remedial materials or software?

What does the classroom teacher recommend?

What does the reading specialist recommend?

What other resources does the school have available?

Is additional help warranted, or can the classroom teacher handle this problem with some minimal help, perhaps some remedial materials already in the building and some guidance from the reading specialist on how to work with these new students, plus strong encouragement?

Does the problem reside with the classroom teacher? If so, what can you, the reading specialist, or others do to help? Is some other action necessary here?

Follow up on any action you take so that you can determine the results of your efforts so far. If you do not get the results you hoped for, ask more questions. Given your resources, what will help? Can you get additional or emergency resources if they are warranted? Are there too many students in the class? What can you do about that?

Within reason, be sure you gather all the data and information you need to address the problem. I say "within reason" because a functioning school is not a research organization, and you can gather only the information that any prudent, intelligent, hard-working administrator can gather.

If, for example, attendance at Back-to-School Night was lighter than last year and the trend seems to be down over three years, make sure you have the "reasonable" data you can gather. How many parents attended each teacher's presentations? (Obviously, you will have needed to ask teachers to keep track of this beforehand.) Look at the data for the past two or three or four years, if they are available. You can ask these kinds of questions:

Are teachers' perceptions correct?

How dramatic is the downward trend?

Do you see any obvious differences from year to year?

Have the hours of the event changed?

Has the student population changed in any way?

Has your publicity for the night changed?

Talk to several teachers, particularly those who live in the community. Phone some parents who attended as well as some who did not to see what they have to say.

The point here is that you need to gather a fair amount of data and anecdotal information before you determine if some change is warranted or required. You don't want to change the day of the week unless many people suggest it, and even then you probably want to do a community survey first to see which evening is best for people. If publicity seems to be the problem, you need to determine the most effective ways within your means to contact parents.

Whatever the program or issue you are tracking, you want to learn as much as you can about strengths and weaknesses. What is good about the science competition program, and what are its weaknesses? You want to get as much current diagnostic information as possible (formative assessment), and at the end you want information on results (summative assessment). It is helpful if the summative information is detailed, that is, gives you information on various aspects of the program or skills that are strong or weak.

Gathering information is just the beginning, although it may be the most time-consuming part of your effort. The next step is to determine what to do with that information. What interventions are likely to lead to good results? The penultimate step is to "measure" the results of your interventions—I put *measure* in quotes because some things are measured statistically, some with a rubric, and others subjectively or anecdotally, that is, from the stories gathered from parents and community members that reveal how people feel and what they believe.

The final step is to determine if the results of any changes you've instituted are satisfactory, given your hopes or goals and the human limitations of what talented, motivated staff members can do under your local conditions. Obviously if the results are inadequate by every reasonable measure, you must implement new efforts that are based on the information and data you have gathered.

RULE NUMBER SEVEN: MANAGE YOUR EXPECTATIONS

You may be getting slightly angry at this point, saying to yourself, "Is this guy nuts? Does he think that every staff member has nothing to do all day but gather data?" I don't think I'm nuts, and I realize that gathering data and information is a small (but important) part of each staff member's work. In every school, teachers and other staff members have all sorts of records and information; the social worker, the English teacher, the guidance counselor, the assistant principal, and all the other staff members already have helpful information in their hands.

My point is not that we should overwhelm staff members with recordkeeping or that the generation of endless data and information is desirable. Frankly, in many places we may have already gone too far with data requirements. However, I do think that much of the data and information can be better organized, better presented, and used more effectively to help teachers and students, and that is what this chapter has been about. Data and information should be our allies, materials that staff members feel are helpful to them in their important work.

When the information becomes either burdensome or confusing, you should intervene quickly. Determine, usually with staff help, what could be eliminated or combined, what could be made clearer, and what information should go to some staff members but not others. You want staff to gather only material that is genuinely helpful and that does not impose an unrealistic burden on the person gathering or receiving the information.

Rules for Statistical Data and Other Forms of Information

1. Determine what data you are receiving now and their value.

2. Determine what data will serve your purpose and who should collect them.

3. Determine what data and information you will require for the school and who should receive them.

4. Determine the best ways to present data.

5. Understand your state's standards, tests, and test result information.

6. Emphasize results in your data gathering and analysis.

7. Manage your expectations.

Keywords

Anecdotal information
Assessment of students
Continual results in schools
Continuous results in schools

Cooperative learning
Data in schools
Presentation of data
Results in schools
School data
School reports
School tests
Statistics and school data
Tests in school

Parents, Community, and Communication

T here are many books and articles on the topics named in this chapter's title—not to mention that parents and other community residents have always been part of the life of a school or district. I'll restrict the information in this chapter to a few good practices that are not very well known or are not used often enough.

Parents are obviously key players in the life of a school. In the early grades, they supervise and help with homework. They sometimes volunteer in the school or raise funds for field trips or equipment, typically through one of the parents' organizations. In every community, parents have skills to contribute, from offering free consulting on technology to baking cakes.

Other community members, who have no children or whose children have graduated from the K–12 system, also can be of great help to the school or district. We certainly need their yes votes on deserving school budgets, and they frequently have skills and information from which the schools can benefit. The keys to keeping your parents and the larger community involved and supportive are communication and inclusion as part of the school support community.

RULE NUMBER ONE: BRING PARENTS AND OTHER RESIDENTS TOGETHER WITH "AREA COFFEES"

The very effective method of communication that I call the area coffee is a great way to bring together members of the school and community in an intimate setting. The following guidelines will get you started.

• Take a look at a map of the area from which you draw your students. Divide the entire area into eight or ten zones or neighborhoods in some logical way. You may want several parents who are already involved with the school to help with this.

• Find a parent in each of the relatively small zones who is willing to host a coffee one evening, perhaps from 7:00 P.M. to 8:30 P.M. Ask the host to invite ten to fifteen neighbors in his or her area with an interest in your school. The host parent or parents need only provide coffee and, perhaps, cake or cookies. Often people who agree to attend will ask what they can bring.

Please note that when I say "parent," I mean to include any legitimate caregiver or community resident. In the first decade of the twenty-first century, it is common for students to live in a single-parent home, for a grandparent to play an important role, or for there to be other "family arrangements." Regardless of how you feel about what constitutes a family, these are the people whose support we need in the school and school community, these are the people who elect board members and vote on budgets, and these are the people who can help the children for whom they are responsible.

• "Advertise" the coffee. It is important to make a general announcement of the zones, hosts, and coffees, so no one feels left out. If a parent or community member is in zone 4, that person should know from a newsletter or e-mail or some other form of communication that a coffee is scheduled for a particular date at Ms. Smith's house or apartment. The community member has the host's phone number or e-mail address, provided in the announcement, and can contact the host to see if there is room for him or her. Hosts should be told at the outset that no one from the community should be turned away unless the group really does exceed the number the host can comfortably have in his or her home. There is always the possibility of repeating the meeting a few weeks later to accommodate the overflow, although this is rarely necessary.

Please note: In some schools, there may be a few students from outside the usual feeder zones. The principal should make sure their families are offered the opportunity to attend a coffee.

• Divide the responsibility. With eight to ten zones and as many coffees, you can't do it all alone. One administrator (principal, assistant principal, department chair, and occasionally a district curriculum person) and one teacher should attend each coffee, although sometimes it is good to have a second administrator or teacher present, particularly when the topic is complex or new.

- Have a stated agenda. There are any number of possibilities for topics, but these gatherings must always have a stated purpose. A coffee might be held to familiarize parents with the new advisory program, a new reading series, or the latest plan to renovate the building, or to help parents understand the new approach to math that the school is taking as a result of some new state requirement.

Informally, of course, things will come up that are not on the agenda, but the administrator or teacher who agrees to take the lead should make every effort to maintain focus on the stated reason for the coffee.

- Take notes. The school representative not taking the lead is the note taker for that coffee. The notes (including full contact information) are important for any follow-up that may be required.

- Brief the principal. The principal should receive a brief report on any neighborhood meeting he or she did not attend. That is another reason why notes are important. At intervals, the principal may wish to bring together all the school representatives who attended these meetings to compare experiences, discuss common issues, and determine how best to proceed.

- Hold perhaps two coffees each year. They can be held as often as needed, but given the demands on staff and parent time, two is about the right number.

Obviously, these events personalize communication and get parents and other residents directly involved in the school. The coffees frequently turn up new people who will help the school in unexpected ways. Of course, you may not locate parents with expertise in some of the areas where you would like help, but often a parent will have a friend or colleague in another school district who can help.

In many schools where this method is used, the host becomes the area conduit for getting information or questions to the proper person in the school. You now have eight to ten people in the community you can depend on to help get word out or to bring you information you might not otherwise hear.

RULE NUMBER TWO: PUBLISH A HIGH-QUALITY NEWSLETTER

Newsletters that are too short, too long, poorly written, or too much at the mercy of well-meaning, busy volunteers with personal agendas are unlikely to be effective. Of course, a newsletter's worst sin is to be irrelevant to its audience, and I say more about that in a moment. The following are some general guidelines for a successful newsletter:

- A school or school district newsletter should probably not exceed six or eight pages on a standard page, typed double-spaced. Of course, it might be slightly longer if it goes out at intervals of four weeks or more.

- The newsletter can be written or edited by a volunteer or a paid person, but whoever does the primary writing and editing (and that might be more than one person) needs to be an excellent writer or line editor. A newsletter with many misspellings and grammatical errors, poor syntax, or incorrect information is not a good advertisement for the school or district. It's a good idea to have more than one person proofread the newsletter before it goes out. Also, do your best to check for accuracy. If in doubt, check again. Stating an incorrect time for an event or mangling a person's name is poor public relations.

- All features of the newsletter should be of high quality. Photographs should be used only if they are clear and if everything of importance in the picture—place, names of people, the title of event—can be stated accurately. Use good-quality paper if the newsletter is mailed or distributed. Many schools now use e-mail, and that is fine.

- Newsletters should go out at regular intervals: every Friday, the last Friday of each month, or six times per year (first week of each quarter, plus two weeks before school starts and one week after school ends). The intervals will depend on your particular needs and the staff available to gather information and write and edit the newsletter. Don't promise a newsletter every week if that is an impossible burden. Regardless of the interval you choose, the intended reading audience should expect to get the newsletter at a particular time. If you do an "extra" newsletter on some unexpected event or major development, be certain that it is worth the effort and will be perceived that way by the reading community.

- It helps readers if there are regular features in each newsletter, such as a principal's message and sections on important dates, volunteers needed, special accomplishments, and school events. In addition, you can have one or two features in each newsletter that do not fit under your usual headings. The Important Dates section would include any information pertinent to those dates, such as what the student should bring on the field trip or the precise time and location of a school meeting or a coffee.

- I can't say it too often: the most important characteristic of the newsletter is relevance. The readers of this newsletter should find it interesting and strongly related to their school concerns. The best compliment is "I always look forward to getting the newsletter because most of it really interests me. My husband and I read it carefully and sometimes even ask our seventh-grader about parts of it."

- If each school has a newsletter and so does the district, the editors should meet once or twice each year to make sure their purposes are different—there should be no unwarranted repetition. There will be some overlap in intended audience, so these issues of purpose and repetition are very important.

- More and more schools distribute their newsletter via e-mail, but do consider those parents, every year becoming fewer and fewer, who do not have e-mail. Do they want to pick up a copy at the school or local library? Do they prefer it to be mailed to them? Be sure to accommodate them.

RULE NUMBER THREE: CONDUCT WORKSHOPS FOR PARENTS

Parents want to know what the school is doing, what is expected of their children, and why something new has been added or substituted in the curriculum. Evening workshops are an effective way to introduce new topics in the curriculum, such as the new reading program in grades K–3 or a revised middle school program on library skills in a technological world. You can also use workshops to cover highly controversial topics, such as how the school plans to handle the teaching of evolution or the new state-required sex education curriculum in a high school health class for sophomores. A well-planned workshop may reduce some of the controversy.

Obviously, conducting workshops is a serious undertaking, so I recommend doing only one or two each year. The workshop can be one or two evenings, but typically it is just one.

The following is an example of a workshop I organized to introduce a new teaching approach. Students were telling their parents about new things they were doing in a schoolwide writing program, and many parents raised questions about the program.

I invited parents to attend a two-evening participatory workshop on the National Writing Project (NWP). The NWP training of our teachers was recent, and students were now approaching writing in a very different way. Many parents were not used to writing groups, say-back, revision, and other features of the new program.

In this workshop, parents went through some of the same processes their children were going through in their writing instruction across the curriculum. The only difference was that parents did not share their work, so the workshop was completely nonthreatening. They saw that their children would write science reports in biology, research papers in social studies, narratives and book reviews in English, and much, much more. They learned that the curriculum was very carefully crafted and quite rigorous, that the writing process yielded far better student work, and, just as important, that the students enjoyed the work. They also read very brief summaries of the research that indicated how successful NWP methods were around the country. The workshops were conducted by teachers, with several students present to help parents.

RULE NUMBER FOUR: INCLUDE PARENTS IN A SITE-BASED SCHOOL COMMITTEE

This rule draws in part from insights gained through my meetings with and writing about Professor James Comer in the 1990s as well as articles on some of Comer's more recent work ("Portrait of James Comer," *Educational Leadership,* September 1990; "Maintaining a Focus on Child Development: An Interview with Dr. James P. Comer," *Phi Delta Kappan,* January 1997). Dr. Comer is a psychiatrist at the Yale University School of Medicine's Child Study Center. He has done a great deal of outstanding work with low-achieving schools, but his ideas and mine apply to all schools. I have blended my own experiences and ideas with some of Dr. Comer's excellent techniques and those of other outstanding practitioners I've observed or met more recently.

• Form a site-based school committee consisting of the host parents or some other representative from each of your school's zones. The committee members can meet among themselves and bring suggestions to the principal; they can meet with the principal or some other designated staff member (assistant principal or teacher); they can meet with a small staff committee, for instance, the principal and two teachers; or they can use some combination of these arrangements depending on the circumstances. This committee will, of course, reflect its own concerns as well as those of friends and neighbors. As with any other committee, there should be a chair (perhaps a revolving one), meetings at regular intervals, and an agenda for at least part of the meeting.

• Set up guidelines for the committee. Committee members need to know right from the beginning what the authority of the committee will be. Whether the principal is going to be a regular member of this committee or not, he or she should be at the first meeting to establish the guidelines, usually working through with the parents the specifics of what those guidelines will be. More is said about the committee's authority later in this chapter.

With the guidelines set, the committee members remain welcome to ask questions about anything at meetings, but the primary purposes of the committee have been established, barring unexpected events. For instance, the committee might have agreed to the following purposes:

Help organize volunteers.

Help staff members with the newsletter.

Serve as a two-way conduit to the larger school community for information gathering and dissemination.

Learn about and comment on new programs, methods, or special events.

Alert the staff members on the committee when something the principal and others should know about is brewing in the community.

Select two members who will meet with the staff committee that selects school-based in-service courses. (These people may or may not have a vote, but their views will be heard and considered carefully.)

Establishing the committee's limitations is delicate work. You want this committee to have several important purposes, but you do not want the committee to dictate curriculum or tell the science teacher how to teach his or her subject. You do not want this committee to usurp the role of the central office, the board of education, or the school's staff, but you do want the committee to know that all their suggestions will be taken seriously, that some of their suggestions will be implemented in some form, and that they will get feedback on what happens to their proposals.

Indeed, some of the things a school committee can do or suggest might be taken up quickly. For instance, if some math professor who often does school consulting is on your committee and volunteers to meet with the math teachers to see if she can be of help, you can probably arrange that. If your custodian is having a difficult time with some individual classroom heating adjustments and your committee includes a very experienced and highly regarded heating repair specialist, you might contact the person in charge of buildings and grounds and arrange for him and your chief custodian to meet with the parent volunteer to see how he can help.

In Chapter Two, Rule Number Six, I discussed establishing a crisis committee and creating a crisis management booklet. Often, parents from the site-based school committee will work on more than one task or committee. Selected parents from the school committee may be helpful adjuncts to the crisis committee. First, one or two parents may wish to serve on the committee to help plan how and under what circumstances parents should play some role, perhaps in disseminating accurate information to their neighbors and squelching rumors. Second, you may have some parents in your community who are social workers or psychotherapists and would be willing to help as volunteers for a day or two in a crisis. Sometimes other parent "specialists" can be of great help in putting together a crisis booklet: for example, a police officer, a physician, a firefighter, a politician, or an educator who works in another district and has gone through a crisis in her school recently or who served on a committee to create a crisis plan.

• Do not underestimate the importance of parents with regard to curriculum. The site-based school committees take on added importance when each school sends two representatives to meet with the curriculum director at two meetings each year. Here is an opportunity, for instance, to inform parents of the mandated programs, especially new programs, and to hear directly from parents what they think and feel about a variety of learning issues. Once again, committee members must be given guidelines so that they know that their proposals will be respected and included as much and often as possible, but at the same time are not misled into believing that this committee will now dictate curriculum or make decisions that the board or a school faculty should make.

Site-based school committees provide an opportunity for the K–12 assistant superintendent for curriculum and instruction or the elementary and secondary curriculum directors to hear that too much or too little homework is assigned in some grades across schools; that homework is not very well coordinated in several schools, resulting in a serious overload for students a few times each year; or that too much or too little time is spent on preparation for state tests. This is also an opportunity for parents to ask questions about the role of state tests in the curriculum, to review when the tests are given, to suggest a topic for one districtwide in-service course for teachers during the coming summer, or to request a workshop for parents on some school topic of considerable interest to them.

If some issues develop that are broadly applicable to the whole community, the central office administrator (assistant superintendent or curriculum director), in concert with school representatives, might wish to present some information in a newsletter or other forum. Many parents these days want to know exactly what the role of state tests will be, how these tests will help their children, what sort of information the tests provide about their individual child and the school, how the test information will be disaggregated, which tests are high-stakes, and other issues related to the testing program. These concerns might be cause for a newsletter on the testing program and a follow-up evening workshop for interested parents.

Rules for Parents, Community, and Communication

1. Bring parents and other residents together with "area coffees."

2. Publish a high-quality newsletter.

3. Conduct workshops for parents.

4. Include parents in a site-based school committee.

Keywords

Comer, James P. (see also the articles mentioned in the chapter)
Comer program
Comer schools
Crisis plans
National Writing Project (NWP)
Parents and schools
Personalizing school communication
School neighborhood groups
School newsletter
Site-based management
Site-based school committee
State tests

Final Thoughts and Advice

Although administrators need to know a great deal of information and possess many specific skills, usually as a result of years of experience in schools, in the end they are hired because the group searching for the new chairperson, principal, or curriculum director thinks a particular candidate will make the *soundest, most mature judgments,* particularly in difficult situations, and will bring the *strongest management or change-agent skills* to the position. This final chapter attempts to buttress the words I've emphasized here as well as highlight a few of the rules presented in this book.

When the search committee makes its final decision, say for an assistant principal's position, it will, to be sure, refer to the specific skills that person possesses or does not possess. In the end, a wise hiring committee will recommend the administrator who best fits its school's idiosyncratic situation and who it believes will make the best judgments across a variety of issues and incidents. In short, by the definition of that school's needs, the committee wants a leader.

To illustrate this, what follows is one case that might be presented to a candidate for the position of assistant principal (AP) in a secondary school where that person will devote some of his or her time to discipline. The committee might even have worked out some guiding questions that it hopes a good (read *capable of sound judgments in this school's circumstances*) AP candidate might raise. Of course, an excellent candidate might make suggestions or propose questions that are different from and better than those listed.

Teacher Jones, angry and hurt by a student's alleged rude defiance in the school hallway, loudly demands that the AP who has just arrived on the scene suspend the miscreant for the maximum time allowed by their state if that AP has an ounce of courage and cares at all about maintaining discipline.

The committee asks the candidate how she would handle this situation and what questions the AP might ask in the hall and later as she investigates what happened.

Committee's Guiding Questions

What do you do on arrival?

How do you defuse the immediate situation?

What exactly did the student do, according to the teacher?

What happened according to the student?

Do you question both parties in the hallway or somewhere else?

Do you question them at the same time?

How can you handle this without alienating the teacher or condemning the student (before you know the full story)?

Are there any mitigating circumstances?

Is the teacher overreacting? If so, does the teacher often overreact this way? Is the teacher a person who very rarely overreacts and is likely to be well justified in acting in this manner?

How should the incident be quickly investigated?

Were any other adults in the area when this incident occurred—a custodian, school aide, teacher?

How do students feel who were on the scene?

Are there other people you need to interview?

Will the teachers' organization become involved in this incident?

Should the student's parents be called? When?

I made this situation somewhat messy, but lots of issues in school life are fairly messy. Over the course of any month in any school, issues arise over budget, test preparation, conference attendance, discipline, faculty meetings, individual or group teacher issues of every sort, staff development, schoolwide mandated and desired changes, schedule, cocurricular activities, tensions between sports and academics, outside pressures from parents, the central office and local leaders, and dozens of other problems and incidents. Many of the situations you will face do not have a default or "correct" answer.

Some issues will be more demanding than others, but the constant is that your maturity and judgment will be tested each day—usually mildly but occasionally sorely. Your ability to make sound, ethical judgments and decisions under all sorts of circumstances, taking into consideration local conditions and, when appropriate, the larger picture, will determine your effectiveness.

Much of this book was intended to alert you to the kinds of dilemmas you will face as well as to give you some sense of the "rules" and possible approaches available to you. I'll leave you with a few final thoughts, at first based on the student incident, that highlight points made in this book.

- No matter what the question or incident, determine as quickly as possible if the situation you are facing is one of great urgency or one that can be played out over time. In the teacher-student example here, you can probably isolate the student from the teacher, perhaps even arrange for the youngster to remain at home for one day without prejudice while you investigate what happened and let the complaining teacher cool down. Another technique, if the incident was not violent or terribly threatening, is to allow the student to remain in school but not go to the complaining teacher's class for two days while you investigate the circumstances.
- Informally and discreetly, let some key people know what you are doing, so that your staff understands that you are gathering information and will decide on a specific course of action in no more than forty-eight hours. In a day or two, particularly if the teacher overreacted and begins to realize that several students and a school aide do not support his version of what happened, your job may to find a way to allow the teacher to save some face and get the student back in class. Of course, you may also end up taking strong disciplinary action if it turns out that the student really did rudely and loudly defy the teacher without any warrant.

When you make your decision, spread the credit around. Be sure that the key people or even the whole staff learns that the school aide or the teacher involved or some teachers' association official was of great help in arriving at an equitable conclusion.

• Always give yourself some time and try to hear from other people before making a decision of any moment. Sometimes you have to act immediately—for instance, when two students are fighting in the hall or a sudden deadline is imposed on you by some authority and cannot be avoided—but more often than not you will have a day or a week or more to determine your course of action. Don't build a reputation as a procrastinator or someone who does nothing and hopes real problems will somehow just fade away, but don't be bullied into overly hasty decisions either. You will soon learn that many people like to give free advice to administrators, and they expect you to act on their advice very quickly. Your job is to determine which people give wise and helpful counsel.

• Acknowledge that each issue that comes up carries with it different time and study requirements. How quickly must you act when several elementary teachers complain that the special area schedule is not working? What about the high school parents who insist that one more AP science course be implemented next semester or year? What do you do about those eighth-grade parents who are beginning to complain that some students have too much free time in their day? How rapidly do you react to the student government request that seniors be allowed more freedom in the school?

• Establish priorities among those issues of considerable magnitude that will influence the school for years to come. How will you determine if an issue should be a priority? Was it mandated by the superintendent or board? Is there strong faculty sentiment about it? Should it be your call? How strongly do you feel about each of the possible priorities? Should you quickly form a small advisory committee to determine which two of the four requests should be identified as priorities? How much do you wish to influence the committee? Should you chair this effort, serve as a committee member, or stay away unless your advice is requested?

• Balance your needs and convictions against the needs and reality of the school or district. You may be a proponent of differentiated instruction, but you realize that the staff in this school must be brought along slowly. How can you begin to seed this concept without causing an uproar in your first or second year on the job? How can you share the responsibility and the credit for any investigation you and the staff undertake with other staff members? Are there some other issues that you feel should not be considered, at least at this time, perhaps because the resources to pursue them are not available or because there are as many major issues under consideration right now as you and the staff can efficiently manage?

- Accept that a functioning school is not a research university and is not set up to undertake large multiyear studies. Those studies have likely been done by universities, and schools can use the findings to help them decide what to do. Teachers and parents (and sometimes district administrators or board members) want to know how and when you'll make your decision. If the decision about, for example, a new program is affirmative, they'll want to know what your school's version of the program will look like, what training will be required, and what the expenses will be.

- Anticipate important issues as well as you can. You know your school and your situation, which is not precisely like any other. Consider what might be hot-button issues at the next budget or discipline or scheduling meeting and some possible responses to those issues. Preparation will take you a long way. Again, consult with several staff members who can give you sound counsel. Your chief custodian may be of great help if minor vandalism is occurring in the school. If there is a problem with test preparation, talk to the English and math teachers who served on the last test preparation committee or study group two years ago.

- Stay in close touch with members of the school community. Regular meetings are important, but do not underestimate informal discussions with custodians, students, parents, teachers, your supervisor, and others. As an administrator, you often need to hear from many people under a variety of circumstances to put parts of the school mosaic together. I recall learning things in parking lot conversations with a custodian or parent or when giving a ride home to a teacher whose car wouldn't start that I would never have learned in a more formal setting.

- Do not let yourself become overwhelmed. This is one of the most debilitating things that can happen to an administrator. You are now in a position where your hours of work, and particularly the hours inside the school building or central office, have been expanded, and many of the responsibilities that you once passed on to your supervisor are now yours to resolve.

When that strong feeling of being overwhelmed afflicts you, and occasionally it will, do something about it early on. For instance, list all the things you need or want to do, and ask yourself these kinds of questions:

Can any of these things simply be crossed out or put off without doing much harm?

Can any items be delegated?

Are there any committees or other work you can give up, at least for a short period?

Can you speak to your supervisor about getting some help, temporary or permanent?

If you feel that you are not working efficiently, is there someone you can ask for help—a friend, a professor, a colleague, an administrator in another district?

Would it help to list things in priority order?

Are the demands of the job unreasonable? If so, you need to think that through carefully and then make your case to your supervisor.

• Seek help from other educators or respected school leadership resources. No situation will be exactly like yours, although you will get your best help from others in similar positions. To the extent possible, spend some informal time with other administrators in your school or district. Go to local area meetings and, if possible, to appropriate state and national meetings. Join one or two professional organizations in your area of work and read articles of particular interest to you in the journals of those organizations. Use the Internet and draw on anyone in your personal or professional network you trust and who can help you. You don't need to feel alone. The more you learn, the more you'll have to draw from when situations arise that require a combination of standard and original thinking.

Your job is not easy, but it is exciting and worthwhile. Many of you, as you gain experience and have success, will mentor younger or less experienced colleagues, write articles, make presentations at meetings and conferences, and even write books that will help other administrators do their work more effectively and efficiently. I have only scratched the surface of what confronts a school leader early in this new century. As you read my book I'm sure you were saying to yourself, "If I were revising this book, I would add x or emphasize y even more." If you are a very experienced administrator, your revisions and additions would be many, and that is fair.

Wherever you are in your administrative career or aspirations, I wish you good fortune, and hope this book has been of some real help! I welcome e-mails telling me what should have been in the book or just stating your views on some aspect of administration. After all, much of what you've just read came from the best of you.

INDEX

29–31; and retreats, 33–36; scheduling, 29–31
Meier, D., 50
Mentors, 9–10
MI. *See* Multiple intelligences
Multicultural education, 24
Multiple intelligences (MI), 25, 50

N

National Association of Elementary School Principals, 21
National Association of Secondary School Principals, 21
National Council of Teachers of English, 21
National Staff Development Council, 21
National Writing Project (NWP), 22, 43, 95
NCLB. *See* No Child Left Behind
No Child Left Behind (NCLB), 25
NWP. *See* National Writing Project

P

Parents, 91–99; and area coffees, 91–93; and newsletter, 93–95; rules for, 99; in site-based school committee, 96–99; workshop for, 95–96
PDK. *See* Phi Delta Kappa (PDK)
Peer coaching, 72
Peer supervision, 72
Personalization, 14–15
Phi Delta Kappa (PDK), 21, 22, 49
Phi Delta Kappan, 7, 21, 49, 96
Police, 15
Policy, safety, 15
Portfolios, 8, 25, 73, 74
"Portrait of James Comer" *(Educational Leadership)*, 96
Problem-based learning, 25, 76

Professional development, 39; courses, 44–45. *See also* Staff development
Professional knowledge, 21–22

R

Recruitment, 5–11; and clear expectations for new position, 6; committee, 5–6; and providing mentor for new hire, 9–10; and researching candidate, 8–9; rules for, 10
Red Lake, 15
References, 8
Renewers, 50
Research, candidate, 8–9
Retention, 5–11; rules for, 10
Retreats, 33–36; characteristics of, 33; and forced choice, 36–37; leaders, 33–36; topics for, 34
Review, 77
Rubric, evaluation, 7–8, 25

S

Safety, 13–19; and personalizing school, 14–15; and protecting emotional well-being, 16–17; and protection from intrusion and disruption, 15–16; regular inspections and, 13–14; rules for, 19; and tracking students, 16
Schwarzenegger, A., 57
Shankar, A., 51
Special interests, 22
Staff development: and compensation, 46–47; course, 42; course planning, 44–45; course relevance, 43–44; focus on manageable goal, 42–43; in-service courses, 44–45; and learning community, 40–42; limiting number of classes in, 45–46; major responsibilities in, 39–40; rules for, 47; and study group, 40–42